This Is China

An Expatriate's Perspective

Written By

RUTH N. STEVENSON

Photography by Natalia Segura

WestBow
PRESS
A DIVISION OF THOMAS NELSON

WestBow Press books may be ordered through booksellers or by contacting:

WestBow Press
A Division of Thomas Nelson
1663 Liberty Drive
Bloomington, IN 47403
www.westbowpress.com
1-(866) 928-1240

ISBN: 978-1-4497-3708-5 (hc)
ISBN: 978-1-4497-3707-8 (sc)
ISBN: 978-1-4497-3706-1 (e)

Library of Congress Control Number: 2012900821

Printed in the United States of America

WestBow Press rev. date: 02/09/2012

Contents

To our families and the people of China, who have inspired us to share our hobbies and our discoveries with the world.

She said:

"But anyone can write a book about their experiences and include pictures of China."

He said:

"True, but can they capture shocking experiences in the moment, before they have become desensitized by years of exposure? You wrote, photographed, and lived . . . in the moment. You took the time to compile it. Only a few can do that, and now you should share it with others . . . with the world."

Enjoy!

Fishing in the City

Preface

Far from a travel guide or anthropological anomaly, the following pages encapsulate one culminating theme: we are all an "other." The ordinary, daily events of one culture may very well be unordinary to another. In a land where most dare not write or photograph reality, we lived, explored, wrote, and photographed life. We searched not for the unusual but for the usual, ironically exposing raw nature and conundrums of normalcy.

The American Heritage Dictionary of the English Language defines *belonging* as "acceptance as a natural member or part." What does it mean to belong? Our innate desire to grapple with being normal and wrestle with unfamiliarity led us to investigate global perspectives as well as our personal environment, China. By analyzing and selecting countless journal entries, anecdotes, voice dictation recordings, and photographs, found within the following pages, a book emerged. This compilation exposes changes in our personal perspectives of Chinese culture as well as our ability and inability to belong.

Exposing the ordinary in China reveals foreign, unfamiliar, and at times, shocking information into the hands of anticipating readers. The following stories are tangible, real experiences that have happened to us, our friends, and citizens of China. If seeking a book that details tourist attractions and luxury accommodations, there are others on the shelf from which to choose. If seeking the alleyways and remote streets of China, a culture truly unknown to most of the world, this book will bring more than reality to your fingertips. It will bring thought-provoking images and pose questions that inspire personal, soul-searching responses.

This conglomeration of information is not intended to demean or belittle life as it is lived in China. On the contrary, *This Is China* seeks to uncover the complexities of humanity as well as expose the lenses through which we view cultural norms. Even after living in China, we would never attempt to claim that we have fully discovered or can adequately display the deep historical and cultural influences that present a true picture of an entire nation. On the contrary, the exigencies of life in China are as unique as the DNA that identifies each of us.

A mere visit or short-term stint through any country reveals exterior images, differing from the internal realities of an authentic ethos. After living in a foreign country, the intriguing novelty of that country often morphs into a concrete understanding of cultural expectations and normalcy and, often, may distort normal, as it was once understood. In this, we find new and exciting opportunities to mature.

Based on one environment, one perspective, in one city, in one province, within one country of more than fifty ethnic subgroups, this entire book is a generalization. However, these perspectives are also honest and justifiable within the current setting. Shenzhen is a fairly new city, having developed from a small, fishing village to a thriving economic hub within a mere twenty years. This, in and of itself, creates volatile and unpredictable societal dynamics. It is our sincere hope that you will allow the text and images to stir feelings deep within.

Acknowledgments

Thank you . . .

John, for sharing life's journey with me as well as continuing to be a husband and father deserving of the utmost respect and admiration.

Claire, for being the best souvenir I could have ever received from our time in China. You bring more joy and love than I will ever be able to adequately describe.

Mom, for always showing genuine interest in my life and pointing me to Truth. I will never be able to adequately describe how grateful I am that you are my mother.

To the other men in my life: Dad, David, Jonathan, and Seth, who have consistently provided strong examples of perseverance and faith.

Laura, for being the best mother-in-law I could have ever hoped for. Our late-night conversations are held treasured in my heart.

Diane, Janet, Brandee, Stacey, Katie, Carol, Kristy, Shelley, Lainey, Andri, Sandra, Alice, Juliette, Natalie, Renee, Theresa, Veerle, Sophia, and Elizabeth, for friendships that are not too often found and ones that I will always hold dear.

Mayla, for providing help to my family and continuing to be someone that will forever be special to me, my daughter, and the entire family.

Without you, this book would have taken more than the four years that it took to complete. Thank you.

Natalia, for sharing your gift with me as well as the world. Your photography captures the moment and inspires people to reflect. Your friendship and this journey will be long remembered with fondness. www.nataliasegura.net

Stanislav, for superior graphic design and stirring photography. It is my hope that your gift may one day be discovered. www. stanislavholota.com

God, for revealing yourself and providing health, strength, and wisdom.

Part I

Creatures of Habits

The Habits

No, not one of us is exempt from habitual activity. If we consider the daily routine with which we greet or bid farewell to the day, it is highly likely that we follow a usual process. In subsequent thoughts, our actions make logical sense. We do not brush our teeth, eat, and go to bed. On the contrary, we eat, brush our teeth, and go to bed because—to us—it is logical. However, is it in fact our *logic* or *custom* that allows us to know the difference between what is habitual, as opposed to what we consider sound reason?

As anywhere, China is full of cultural customs and habits that have become embedded in the very nature of the population. At first glance, these habits may appear odd and, at times, a bit offensive. Yet within these customary behaviors and ways of life, we can find interesting connections to the "survival of the fittest" philosophy as well as the pragmatic "means to an end" mentality. Do we have habits because they inspire routines which make life easier? Do we do things because they lead to efficiency? *Efficiency* . . . what does it mean to be efficient? Do our habits reflect proper use of time? Do we waste time to guard against possible impressions? As the following journal entries reveal, habits infiltrate and become the acceptable and unacceptable aura of an ethos.

March 8, 2008—Illogical or Logical?

I spent most of today reading, but I ventured out to the gym for an hour. In the elevator, you would think that the world was moving too slow. As soon as someone steps onto the elevator, people in

China frantically push the "><" symbol, indicating that the door is closing. As soon as someone steps off the elevator, they frantically push it again. To me, it appears to be an action of impatience, but I have been told that, to the Chinese people, it means no more than, "Okay, that person is where they need to be, now let's get on with the show." I chuckled at myself today; as soon as someone exited on their floor and I was by myself, I frantically pushed the "> <" symbol to close the door. Although no one was with me to witness my behavior, I knew that I had done something that would be familiar to the Chinese, yet somewhat odd to those in the States. How do our environments shape our behavior? Are we quick to judge or quick to adopt new practices?

June 24, 2008 — It landed twenty centimeters from my foot!

Luohu is a unique place and one of Shenzhen's busiest districts. I can't say that I have ever visited a place quite like this, and now I am living in the heart of it. I live three blocks from the train station and three blocks (in the opposite direction) from Dongmen. Here is what happened today: As I walked past the shops, hand clutching my bag, I could feel the eyes of each shop owner as I looked for anything familiar. I was on my way to a place called Dongmen. I was told that I could find "anything I wanted" there. I began to see that this area was definitely a conglomeration of supplies. With pictographs above each open-aired entrance, I had to depend on my eyes to peruse the merchandise. The shops were side by side, each protected by metal doors that rolled down like garage doors at closing time. It was true; each shop displayed different products. I saw everything from an entire shop of hair accessories to a shop with countless Halloween costumes (mind you, in June). Where had I landed? I had never been anywhere where I could potentially buy a towel for my bathroom, get a massage, buy a moped, and have my pants hemmed . . . all within the same strip of shops. Yes, we have "supercenters" back home where people can have their oil changed while purchasing school supplies and checking off the grocery list, but these individual shops held hundreds, maybe even thousands, of one item.

Although this place might be good for shopping, I can't say that I was pleased with every part of my experience.

As I walked, I kept hearing the same sound, over and over again—the sound of someone "hawking a loge." Now for those who do not know this term, it refers to the noise made by clearing the throat of mucus, propelling it up the esophagus into the mouth, and emitting it out of the mouth by spitting with force so as to prevent the contents from landing on the shirt. For some, this is associated with intense sports; athletes must clear their esophagus from unnecessary debris. However, I was not on a sports field. I was in a busy marketplace.

Over and over again, I heard this sound coming from not only the common people on the street, but also shop owners. The sound came from young and old, male and female alike. It was as though people on this street had mucus in their mouths and they were trying—no, *determined*—to get it out of their mouths. At one point, a man on a bicycle whizzed past me, only to emit his spit within centimeters of my open-toed shoes. My immediate reaction was that of disgust. How revolting! Why must they spit out in the open? Don't they know that this is rude and discourteous to those around them? Don't they know that bacteria lives in spit, and this creates an ideal environment for an epidemic? Why are they spitting at me? Some people even looked directly into my eyes and, having felt some sort of satisfaction with my attention, proceeded to "hawk" with full force! I feel as though I should call this area "spitmen" rather than "dongmen." Again, I have not come to understand if these people are ill or if this is some kind of annoying habit. I find myself wondering if I have been exposed to enough of this to know if it is, in fact, a typical Chinese mannerism. Only time will tell.

March 9, 2009—And, yes, he spat on my floor!

Today I was in our new apartment on the thirtieth floor, painting the walls. For the past week, I have been busily preparing for our move to Shekou, a convenient expatriate area where it doesn't even feel as though I am in China (as compared to my experiences in Luohu). Here, there are many people who speak English, and grocery stores have a few familiar imported brand-name products. Around 2:30 this afternoon, the man who was installing a light fixture arrived. He climbed on a chair but he was too short to reach the ceiling, and I didn't have a ladder. In a hilarious game of charades, he was able to explain that he wanted to move the table from its current location to where he could climb on it to install the light. After numerous grunts and hand motions, we were ready. The scene: table with cardboard pieces protecting the wood . . . chair on top of cardboard pieces . . . paint can on top of chair . . . Chinese man on top of paint can . . . light fixture in Chinese man's hand. After three attempts and two holes in my ceiling, the fixture is hanging above the living room, but I am not sure how long it will hold.

(Two-and-a-half years later, the fixture is still in place and the extra hole is still visible.)

After this, he proceeded to climb down from the paint can, chair, and table and walk to the hallway. As I was moving the paint can back into the guest room, I heard the all-too-familiar sound. YES! It was the sound of hawking as well as a loogie hitting my floor! *Splat!* What was he thinking? This was not the outdoors. This was not a work zone. Yes, I was remodeling, but the apartment was still clean! I feel bad now, as I sit here and reflect on my actions, but I was livid. I began to yell in English about how spitting was completely and utterly inconsiderate and that he should leave now, with his spit and the tools that had left holes in the ceiling! I can't find words to describe how I felt and still feel! Would anyone here possibly understand me if I tried to explain it to them? I fumed as I worked at disposing of this bodily fluid without contaminating myself. Another day . . . another story.

October 3, 2008 — Dispose of it.

I have learned that spitting is rather common in China and comes with a variety of explanations. Today, a traditional Chinese man told me that there are multiple health benefits to spitting. I asked him what they included. He elaborated on the cleansing nature of spitting. "Those that spit are getting rid of anything bad that is in the body. Many people breathe the air from the cars, and they must not allow it to stay in their body. Spitting helps them get rid of the dirt." He continued by explaining that spitting allows them to take any of the 'bad germs' that they get from their neighbors and dispose of them. After explaining multiple situations in which I felt as though they were directing their mucus in my direction, he explained a unique prospect. He asked me, "Have you ever noticed if the people who appear to be spitting at you are old?" I said I hadn't ever paid attention to the age of the people who were seemingly hawking their loogies in my direction. He told me something that I can't stop thinking about, and I have to wonder if this is his own somewhat mythical folktale that has been passed down from generation to generation in some small circles of Chinese customary beliefs. In some ways, it makes perfect sense — yet in others, I find it utterly ridiculous.

He explained, "Many older people say that demons live in the mucus of foreigners. When they see someone who is from the West, they spit to ensure that demons do not pass through the mucus of the foreigner into their own bodies. They believe that these demons can only be avoided by emitting mucus from their mouths. That's why you may feel as though they are spitting at you; they are simply trying to keep your demons away from themselves." I asked this man if he believed this tale, and he explained that his Christian faith has kept him from believing such things, yet he knows many people in his hometown who believe this to be true. Anything that is foreign should not be trusted and carries with it the unknown. Interestingly, although I can't say that I agree with the idea of demons living in my spit, I find myself thinking about the germ pool here. I have been exposed to germs which are quite unique from the germs I experience in my native country. I suppose there are things that have challenged my immune system and given my body a workout. Although I am not sure I have ever felt the urge to spit, I have felt the urge to hold my nose for periods of time, trying to keep whatever is "out there" from coming inside. Interesting. Is my nose-holding the same reaction as their spitting? Should I be spitting? Should I be getting rid of the dust, dirt, and germs that may be inside? Should I adopt the motto, "when in China . . ."? I am not sure if I can. These are habits and customs which are deeply embedded in an entire culture. My culture typically frowns on public spitting. Can I begin to break these cultural norms as I know them, or can I act one way in one place and another somewhere else? These are all questions with which to grapple.

China's visceral practicality is the result of years upon years of survival. China is now a developing country, but the past is a clear picture of underdevelopment and overpopulation. The customs and habits are often associated with surviving—doing whatever is necessary to reach the next day, unharmed, sheltered, fed, and clothed. As a recently developing country, many traditional views and customs still abound. Health statements and proclamations are now leading the more educated people in China to recognize facts and research regarding hygiene and behavior. Since the severe acute respiratory syndrome (SARS) outbreak in 2002, additional precautions have been taken to inform people. In the years following the outbreak, wearing masks decreased the spread of infectious disease and became quite common for those who were ill or working in public areas. Today, revelations continue to increase awareness and prompt paradigm shifts in a few of the customs that relate to bodily functions.

One of these, of which it is hard to write, is public urination. It is hard to write about this because it may appear crude and, at times, boorish and disrespectful. However, in China it is a standard practice—a habit, an accepted behavior—which may change drastically in the coming years. As China develops, there will come a time of confrontation between that which is acceptable and hygienic, and that which is not. In this, we will find many answers to the question, "What is acceptable, normal, and cultural, as it applies to a global community?"

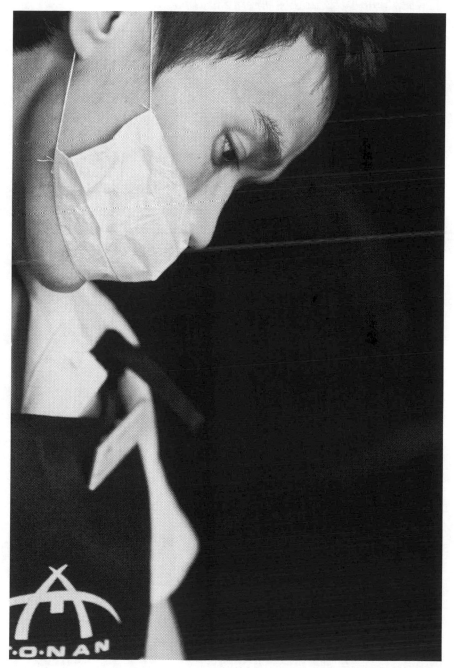

mask,worn to protect

September 12, 2009—Peeing and pooing in the street . . . easy.

Today, I embarrassed my husband. I was trying to snap a photo of something that continues to amaze me: the way in which any public place is considered to be fair space for a latrine. It is quite common to see children urinating in drainage systems lining the roads or in the green spaces along the playgrounds. Children are taught to relieve themselves as necessary in the closest available green space or culvert. Grandparents, who are often the caregivers in China, are frequently seen holding a child, bare-bummed, above a grated ditch or cardboard remnant. The grandmother usually sits on a stool, legs apart, and holds the legs of the child forty-five degrees apart so that the pee and/or poo will reach its desired target. Now, I fully understand the convenience of going whenever and wherever it is necessary. There is an odd sense of luxury at being able to expedite the process of relieving oneself by simply going, on demand, anywhere, anytime. I, too, have had to relieve myself while hiking on a trail where I may have been at least five miles from a toilet. Of course, in these times, a toilet is not readily available. However, I find it odd that in a city as large as this, people continue to find it quite acceptable to urinate or do additional "personal business" along the streets. To make things more interesting, young children's garments accommodate this acceptable habit. Yes, there is a slit (rather, a wide hole) in the crotch of each pair of trousers. Intentionally, the fabric is sewn in such a way that the entire "personal space" is exposed. This makes it easier for the child to "go." This is what I wanted to capture on film.

For me, it is quite odd to see parents and grandparents walking around with bare-bummed children—often bums which are pushed up against the arm of the carrier, waiting for a shower, or worse, to cascade down. Children walk around with their private areas exposed to the air. Today, I wanted to get a picture of the slit in clothing. We were in a place called Sea World, which is not a place where we could see dolphins, whales, and other sea creatures as we originally thought (another long and funny story, but no time here). No, it was a shopping/dining area, and there were hundreds of people milling around. As we walked toward an enormous statue of a mermaid, I could see ahead of us—a slit! I instantly reached for my camera. If I could just take a good picture, my parents might understand more about that which I had been describing to them. This child moved quickly, and it had to have been obvious that I was trying to take a picture of his behind. It is not easy to be inconspicuous when it requires the right angle to capture such a scene. I pretended to be watching the tug-of-war game that was going on between two rather large groups of Chinese men. However, behind the spectators, I was hunched down, pointing the camera at "the slit." My husband's eyes said it all: *You have lost your mind, taking a picture of a child's bottom!*

Is my fascination with this acceptable habit/cultural norm so odd? It is something so completely foreign to me. If we purchased something with a hole in the bottom, we would think it was defective. However, if they were to purchase something without a hole, they may be under the impression that the factory forgot to remove the crotch. What a concept! Are they wise to be so practical and logical in excluding this fabric that gets in the way? Back home, mothers purchase garments with snaps on the bottom to easily reach the diaper area. Without snaps in these slits, efficiency is heightened. Is the slit somehow another level of efficiency, in which the business at hand may be accomplished more effectively? This is an interesting idea. This simple norm may help make lives more fundamentally easy.

September 14, 2009—Soooo, I asked.

Rather than speculating on the reason for the frequent urination and slitted-garments, I asked Sunny (a Chinese friend) about these habits. She elaborated:

"Ruth, it's the easy way. For the first part, 'going' in the streets is sometimes the only place that a person can go. It is better that they are going in the bushes or in the ditch, because they are still, in some ways, being 'nice' about it. If you have to go, and you have no time or nowhere to go, it is better to take care of business, right? You know, Ruth, we do not believe in diapers. They are bad for the skin. Who wants to sit in their wet pants? For babies, it is unhealthy for them to sit in a diaper. We do not think that people should sit in their pee. Is this okay for Western cultures? We only use diapers if we are in very busy public places. The children in China, I think, learn to go to the toilet by themselves much faster than other children in the world. I think they learn not to like the feeling of going on themselves. Maybe it is a good thing we can share with the West. Maybe they would like to try this way. Then, they may not have a hard time potty-training their children."

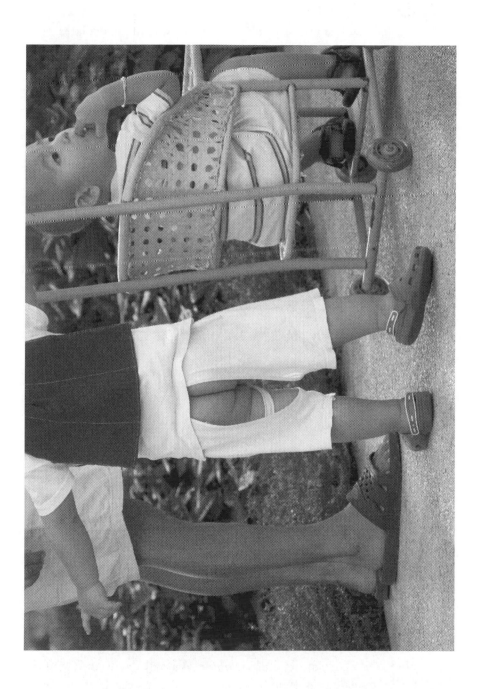

I was stunned by her words. Yes, maybe she is right. Have we forgotten that this was probably the original way in many places throughout our world? Why do we do the things we do? Do we do them because they are better for us? Do we do them because they are more convenient? Do we justify our actions if we think we are doing something better than someone else or with more efficiency? How funny that we might be so quick to judge the actions and habits of a culture that is possibly staying true to rooted habits and customs. Although I have concluded that both children and adults should not continue to relieve themselves in the streets, when there are adequate facilities available, there may be some interesting aspects of childhood training that come from Sunny's comments.

October 4, 2008 — Finally . . . remodeled.

My husband: "They remodeled the restrooms in the office building."

Me: "Really? What improvements did they make?"

Him (with a smirk): "They removed the Western toilet and put in a new squatter."

Me: "What? Why?"

Him: "I was told the men are trying to stand up on the toilet seat to squat, and it is quite dangerous."

Me: "No way! First, the slits for convenience and now the removal of Western toilets for safety. What is next?"

The "squatters," otherwise known as toilets, are conveniently placed in the ground so that squatting is made easy. They are made of corrugated porcelain and quite common. Actually, it is only within the last fifteen years that divider walls have been placed between each squatter. Upon visiting China, it is one of the most shocking aspects, and there are numerous stories that could fill these pages. One such story is undated, yet unforgettable.

Date Unknown — The linebacker.

Imagine a six-foot-five, two-hundred-sixty-pound, former collegiate linebacker from Philly who has just landed in China. It's probably difficult to see how this person could fit in China, much less in normal clothing. He is a giant among them. The story has it that this massive man happened to be the Vice President of Sales for a company, and he settled into a meeting with several vendors. During the meeting, the urge to use the bathroom crept upon him. Fortunately, this happened prior to the Western toilet being replaced with the squatters. What this guy soon discovered, as most first-timers to China have, was that restrooms do not typically stock toilet paper. Most nationals carry tissue in their handbags or briefcases for such occasions. Suddenly, Bob (whose name has been changed to protect his identity) returned to the meeting room with noticeable sweat beads budding along his hairline. Frantically, he grabbed a roll of toilet paper from the four-foot-six, eighty-five-pound receptionist and returned to the restroom. In America, while cleaning, janitors usually close off restrooms, or they simply wait until patrons have vacated the area before mopping the floors. However, this is China. Cleaners do their jobs with little or no regard for others. After mopping one stall, the janitor commenced mopping the stall occupied by Bob. Shoving his mop underneath the door, Bob could only defend himself by kicking the mop away. Finally, having thought the ordeal was over, Bob stepped from the stall to wash his hands. Almost immediately, the Chinese man began screaming at him. Caught off guard, Bob began screaming back at the Chinese man, which he so easily dwarfed. The Chinese man screamed louder and pointed to the stall from which Bob had emerged. It was at this point that Bob noticed a flood of water and sewage gushing from the toilet. Obviously, he also did not realize that used toilet paper is typically disposed of in the wastebasket.

It is a relief (no pun intended) to know that adults do not have slits in their clothing. Most people are adequately clothed with as little exposure to the sun as possible. The *type* of clothing is a different matter. Many people in America might sneak to the mailbox in their bathrobes, hoping not to be discovered by an onlooking neighbor. Casual attire has also taken on a new look in America with sweatpants and the I-just-woke-up-and-rolled-out-of-bed look. I have also heard mothers with multiple children say, "I always hope that I won't have an accident or be pulled over on the way to school, because sometimes I am still in my house shoes." However, if a person were to go to the grocery store in their pajamas, he/she might receive funny looks. Here, the middle-aged and older generations frequently wear pajamas in public. On any given morning or night, along the coastline of Shenzhen, multiple men and women can be seen shuffling along in a pair of pajamas. The most interesting scene, though, is to witness a lovely lady in pajamas, holding an umbrella.

April 21, 2009 — The umbrellas (rain or shine).

Summer is approaching, and the umbrellas are coming out. I shouldn't be surprised, as each summer the umbrellas seem to arrive from every direction. Today, I saw a lovely lady in her pajamas. From a distance, I had seen that she was holding an umbrella. What struck me as I drew closer was that she was holding her umbrella to protect herself from the harsh sun, yet she was already standing in the shade of a tall apartment complex. After that, I noticed it more and more. Everywhere I went, today, there were people holding umbrellas, and regardless of the crowds or shading, the umbrellas were up. At one point, a girl pushed her way to a shaded area with her umbrella, forcing others who did not have an umbrella, to go around her into the sunlight. I watched with interest and confusion.

I recall from my history books that many women in the nineteenth century tried to prevent sun exposure, as the pigment of the skin might darken and give the impression that they were manual laborers. To be fair-skinned was desired, and parasols were carried to help ensure that the skin was covered and protected. Now, in most Western countries, many people desire to be tanned, exuding a healthy glow. Is it always that we want the opposite of what we have? Why? Why do we yearn for that which is in opposition to our natural beauty? It should not be.

Interestingly, the stores in China are full of whitening creams and facial masks that guarantee whiter skin in two weeks. It reminds me of the dental hygiene sections back home, where teeth-whitening creams line the shelves. I imagine that the opposite of a spray tan would do quite well in China. Is there any way I could invent a spray-whitening system? Sure, the white airbrush might wear off, but so does a spray tan in the West. I have heard three different Chinese theories on why almost everyone here carries the umbrella: 1) Western advertisements primarily use fair-skinned models; therefore, this is what China believes is the desired look; 2) to have lighter skin is to proclaim the status in the working sector that you are not a laborer who works in the sun; and 3) there are health risks with exposure to the sun.

Regardless of the reasons, the umbrellas were out in full force today, and I have a feeling that they won't be gone any time soon. I wonder if I should begin to carry an umbrella. I have already begun to question a few freckles on my body. It might be a good idea to take extra measures . . . . but, probably not to the extent that I stand in the shade with my umbrella up.

October 3, 2011—Don't laugh, but . . .

I knew it would happen. How could it not? After living here long enough, we simply let down some of our guards and adopt a few of the same habits. We adapt . . . then adopt. Yes, this morning, I greeted the smile of a familiar expat. It was just past 8:00, and she was out walking her dog. The funniest part: I didn't even notice that she was in her pajamas (a cute matching set) until she said, "Don't laugh, but I just decided if they feel comfortable doing it, so should I. I needed to walk the dog, so here I am. I don't think anyone will even notice or care." I laughed. She is right. Sometimes, when we are completely out of place, we do things that will make us feel more like we belong. Although I know this wasn't her motive, how often do we consider our actions in light of this concept of belonging? Do we do things in one environment that we would never contemplate doing in another?

Something as simple and basic as taking care of our bodily needs can have deeply embedded cultural expectations. We are expected to behave according to the expectations and guidelines that are set by our native culture. We qualify acceptable and unacceptable behavior as it relates to our personal biases and teachings. What, then, can we say about "the other"? That they are somehow wrong in their ways? Who determines if they are wrong? What habits are good? Is research and discovery the truth of what is good or bad? In China, the age-old customs and practices are rooted in tradition and word of mouth. For those who are pregnant, the rules take a personal, more emotional, place of honor. For most, these Chinese traditions are at the heart of their beliefs and customs. Within this set of deeply traditional behavior, I met serious confrontation.

February 8, 2009—Stop wearing your contacts.

I don't know whether to laugh or cry. With my hormones in a constant state of flux, I think it would be best for me to simply have a good, long, hard cry. Less than twenty minutes ago, I had four women sitting in my apartment, explaining all of the things that I am doing wrong in my pregnancy. I am almost four months along, and I have just begun to feel normal, as the first trimester was filled with constant trips to the porcelain throne with ceaseless nausea. This is my first child, and I have nothing to compare this pregnancy to in China—let alone what it is like to carry a child in my native country. All I know is what I am experiencing here, and I have obviously been doing everything wrong.

parasol of the 21st century

pajamas…acceptable public attire

I learned that I should not be wearing any makeup, as it is extremely bad for the baby's skin. I also learned that I should not wear blue jeans, as this is also harmful for the baby. I tried to explain that I was wearing maternity blue jeans with an elasticized waist, but they did not want to hear what I had to say about this. In addition to my harmful choice of trousers, I was told that wearing contacts have a negative impact on the baby's eyes, and that I should never, under *any* circumstance, have an ice cream cone. "The ice cream is cold, and it will be very bad for the baby inside because it will make the baby cold; the body has to work too hard to warm up the ice cream." I didn't dare tell them that ice cream was one of the items that I craved and enjoyed at least three times a week. I should never wear heels, as this would also be bad for the baby. I understand the practicality of not wearing heels, especially in a country where most of the pavement is uneven and/or made of marble (extremely slippery when wet), but to explain that it is bad for the baby is quite a misconception. In addition to these rules, I was told that I must not eat spicy food or drink any beverages with ice. The spicy food will cause the baby to have darker skin, and the ice will, again, make the baby cold.

After their list of rules and examples of when I had failed to follow the rules, their intervention continued with an explanation of which fruits I should be eating. Of course, they brought the fruit with them, and I was given mandarin oranges and apples. The last thing that they wanted me to do was wear a vest. I had seen this vest on multiple Chinese women, and I knew that it indicated pregnancy. Many times, the front of these vests appeared dirty, as if they had been worn multiple times without washing between wears. The ladies, so "politely" sitting in my home and helping me adjust my ways during pregnancy, explained that the vest would protect the baby from exposure to harmful energy waves from the computer, microwave, mobile phone, or any other electronic devices. I sat in awe. My husband had told me that the women at his office would ask a colleague to heat their lunch in the microwave while they stood in another part of the office, so as not to be within "harmful distance" of the microwave in which their food was being heated. Wow! They were really serious about the idea that this vest, which looked much like a painter's smock, would keep their unborn babies protected from the radiowaves, yet the hospitals boasted rooms, marked in clear English: "abortion room."

Where am I? How can these ladies expect me to believe all of these rules and follow these extremely foreign guidelines? I don't think women back home follow these same rules and, if so, I have never heard of any of these things. Of course, I have heard that natural is better and to be careful about what you put on your skin while you are pregnant as there may be things in lotions and or cosmetics that are not as natural as we think, and I have been aware that eating healthy is extremely important, whether you are pregnant or not. However, to think that drinking cold items will harm the baby or having poor eyesight is somehow void of any genetic foundation is completely new and confusing. How could I have begun to explain to these women that their traditions, beliefs, understandings, and "mother-to-daughter" advice was wrong? I feel stuck right now. Lost. Unable to fathom how this could be! Actually, I am feeling so utterly down right now, as if I have been given the news that I am doing the worst things for my baby.

(three hours later)

There is no logical reason that I should stop wearing contacts for the sake of my baby's eyes or worry about what fabric I'm wearing. Top geneticists have studied how traits are passed from one generation to the next, and never in their thousands of studies have they determined that wearing contacts or eating ice cream or wearing maternity blue jeans will be detrimental to the development of the unborn child. Therefore, there is noteworthy advice, and there are just folktales. An example of a noteworthy claim is that too much alcohol will affect the baby or smoking leads to possible premature deliveries. These are based on medical studies and quantitative research. In these circumstances, the facts are clear, but simple generation-to-generation banter cannot lead me to think that I am somehow inept at carrying a child. Wow! Words carry power. Have you ever stopped to think about how deeply rooted the seeds of life-lessons have been sewn? What do you believe to be a fact, regardless of what has been studied or reported? To what extent do we even trust science to be accurate? To whom or what do we go for advice, wisdom, and counsel? This is, above all, what we are talking about here. Various cultures have been exposed to various belief systems. What we believe and/or trust is based on the influential factors in our neighborhoods, in the media, and in our homes.

Interestingly, these cultural norms and expectations are alive and real—to the point that I am baffled by logical connections between hygienic and traditional status quo. Generally speaking, Chinese women who have had a caesarean section are expected to rest for thirty days. In many cases, these women are instructed not to bathe or get their hair wet. This is to guard against infection and to ensure proper time for healing. Under no circumstances are these traditionalists permitted to go outside. Therefore, the first thirty days after delivery is spent without much movement. To be expected, there are exceptions to this practice, but the majority of people do not think this is odd or remotely unhealthy. In their eyes, this is the best way to ensure a full recovery. Through our lens, this may appear impossible or absurd. How could we possibly rest for thirty days without going outside or bathing? If we recognize that our way is based on what is expected in our environment, can we assume that our way is better?

Are we naïve to think that all women in China labor in a private room, are discharged in one to three days, go home to their families, and begin working again in six weeks? Do we know that some women in Europe are allowed to keep their jobs (without pay, of course) for up to two years after their baby arrives, returning to a "same-level" position? Do we see the world as it is, or do we see our neighborhood as it is, maybe our city, our state/province, or country? Do we need to expand our views? We have all—yes all—morphed into our own form of "normal." We have expectations, which are based on experience and years of exposure to an ever-changing world. Again, this is the exposure of the vast difference with which we experience "normal" in our differing cultural practices. Regardless, we live in a world where we can choose to open our eyes and discover or close them and remain dormant. What have we seen today? What did it teach us? Be mindful.

June 14, 2009—Summer is here; shirts up!

I'm not the only one who rubs my belly. Yet, I feel as though I have a good reason to pat my stomach in an occasional, circular motion; I have an obvious presence . . . a life inside. I am pregnant! Today, as on many typical sweltering, summer days in Shenzhen, I saw two large groups of men walking with their shirts pulled halfway up their torsos. With midsections exposed, most of them lean back in a casual sort of swagger as they walk, all the while caressing and patting their stomachs. Imagine, a group of Chinese men, probably most in their mid to late forties, shirts raised to their chests, rubbing and patting their midsections. They appeared overtly casual, sun blaring down on their shiny stomachs, with not an inkling that anyone might think this was strange or uncouth. No. Here, walking around with exposed bellies is a highly acceptable way in which they stay cool. If I were to walk down the street in Barnesville (the small Georgia town from which I moved), I would not see anything remotely similar. No, I might see a sign that says "no shirt, no shoes, no service," but the idea of more than five men walking around with exposed belly buttons might even cause an uproar. It might possibly even qualify as a public disturbance. Why? Because we are not used to this scene.

As I sit and reflect on my reactions to these men, I chuckle. They were minding their own business, unaware and unscathed by their surroundings. They were completely at ease because no one thought their actions to be odd or strange, and why would they? To be honest, no one but the foreigners living here would notice. Why would they pay attention to something so logical? If you are hot, raise your shirts. An expat, having lived in China, will read this and recall with a smile the many times they have witnessed this scene or laughed at the strutting bellies that lined the sun-filled streets. The Westerner who reads this will simply sit and envision a scene and/or behavior that is far removed from contextualization.

What are you used to? Do you have habits? What do you see on an everyday basis that shapes your familiarity? Do you pass the same grocery store or go to the same coffee shop on your way to work? Do you open your refrigerator every day and know exactly where to find the milk—so much so, that you could reach for it and find it when you've lost power and it is dark? What if you woke up tomorrow, got in your car, and drove the same route, only to find that the coffee shop was gone? What if, in its place, was a fruit stand? Instantly, your world would feel as though it had been thrown for a loop. You might feel bewildered, aghast, perplexed, inquisitive, and quite possibly, frustrated. When faced with change and modifications to what has become a normal part of life, the result stirs complex emotional and metaphysical responses. This is what it is like to experience China. This is what it is like to live in China. This is China.

May 2008—Twelve to two, honka . . . chooooo.

I kid you not. With the exception of three people, everyone in the office has a pillow in his/her drawer. Today, I decided to join my husband for lunch. Upon arriving at the office just past noon, I noticed that it was unusually quiet. I peered inside to ensure that I had alighted on the correct floor, and I could see the familiar company logo posted above the reception desk. I didn't see the receptionist, so I continued past the desk toward the back of the office. The sound of fingernails tapping keyboards as well as noodle bowls being slurped broke the silence, but there was no typical office chatter. As I walked through the central area, I saw many of the merchandisers sitting in their desk chairs with heads on top of pillows that had been placed on their desks. My first thought was: *Is everyone ill?* Then I wondered how they could possibly be comfortable sleeping in that position. Upon finding my husband, I asked, "What is going on? Is everyone okay?" Come to find out, for many traditional Chinese, 12:00 to 2:00 is the time for eating and resting. It reminds me of naptime in Kindergarten.

Fruit

shoes, always left at the door

In my adult years, there have been many times that I wished for a standard naptime. What I would have done to have naptime in college. Right after lunch is usually when I was most drowsy. All I can think is: *why don't we have naptime in America?* This is a great idea! One of the ladies who works in the office was able to answer my question. Me: "So, do you take a nap, too?" Her: "Yes, I usually take a nap from 1:00 to 2:00. I have my pillow in the top left drawer." She showed me her pillow. I couldn't believe it—a pink Hello Kitty pillow. Me: "So, did you know that I would never have been allowed to take a nap on the job?" Her: "Really? Well, we have been so busy lately that many of us need to stop sleeping. I know the company would rather us keep working, so I think things are changing here."

And they did change; now in 2011, no one in the office naps from 12:00 to 2:00).

As I sit and ponder images in my mind, I think of the copious number of men I have seen sleeping in every imaginable place: in the back of a cart, on benches, straddling drainage grates, on top of flattened cardboard, under trees, on bamboo scaffolding, in the shovel of a bulldozer, on the bus, in a basket, on the subway train, and even leaning precariously against a concrete wall, all the while atop a bicycle. Many people in this country sleep during the hottest part of the day. Have you ever taken a pillow to your office? Have you ever rested during the day? Have you ever wanted to? Interesting habits are formed by necessity as well as expectations and tradition. What habits have you formed? How are they similar or different from the habits you had as a child under your parents' roof?

Everyone exhibits some form of habitual behavior and mannerisms. It is because of these habits that we can easily function in a life of often chaotic, unpredictable experiences. We cope with a variety of circumstances by accessing and utilizing the norms we have created within ourselves to defuse frustration or insecurities, and so on. Habits help us feel connected and familiar with our environment. Even after being here so long, I often feel disconnected from many of the habits within China. These habits are unfamiliar and odd to me. For instance, on morning or evening walks, I couldn't understand why so many men and women, especially of an older generation, would appear to beat and slap themselves. I elaborate:

October 18, 2009 — Circulation or psychopath?

Really, what *are* they doing? I can't tell you how many times I have gone for a walk and witnessed people beating themselves. I see woman after woman, balling her hands into fists, pounding herself in the rear or along her arms. I can't say that I have ever seen anything like this! Similarly, I often see men swinging their arms back and forth, toward and away from their faces. As the hands come toward the face, they often slap themselves on the chest or the bicep area of the arm. Every time I see them slapping their chests, I can't help but hear Tarzan yodeling his familiar yell in my mind. If it were just one or two people, I might think they were odd, but I counted at least eight people who were hammering themselves with their fists and/or palms tonight.

from 12:00-2:00

If this type of behavior were witnessed at home, we would think something had gone seriously wrong with the brain synapses. However, this is so distinctly common here, that I have come to understand its normalcy. For the older generation, it appears to be a sacred routine. Imagine, you take a walk and everyone you see over the age of sixty is steadily plodding along while thumping him or herself. Why? What benefit comes from this activity? Should I be beating myself, too? As I sit and watch my three-month-old daughter sleep, I wonder if she will grow up in this unique environment. Will she be the one to think beating oneself is normal? In America, one day, will she think it is odd that everyone walks about with straight arms?

China is full of interesting mannerisms. The people in China understand the body in a way that most do not. They are in tune with internal and external connections. Circulation and balance takes a high position on the list of health priorities. When we gently and repeatedly pat our arms, our arms become somewhat red or pink. In China, stimulating the body involves lightly beating, slapping, thumping, and patting. Many people believe that this will increase the flow of blood and decrease symptoms of rheumatism, arthritis, and high blood pressure. Behind every habit, there is a reason for such behavior and, whether scientific or strictly cultural, it is quite often deeply ingrained! These habitual mannerisms are entrenched and supported by holistic acceptance. If everyone is doing it, it must be okay, right? If no one thinks it is gross, then it can't be gross, right? If the majority thinks it is disgusting, it must be disgusting, right? At home, the majority thinks that putting your finger in your nose is unsuitable and sordid; yet, this is China, and the pinky fingernail has been given a distinguished place of honor in the nose.

I must preface the following anecdote with a cautionary reminder: generalizations are dangerous. It must be understood that there are many people in China who will also feel that the following fairly common habit is unacceptable and, to be honest, revolting. Having come in contact with many people who are conscientious of health and hygienic standards, an all-encompassing generalization is unfair and inaccurate. As in any culture, there are always exceptions to what is apparently the norm or ordinary behavior. It is with this in mind that the reader should continue.

Early Morning

March 2011—Status or status quo.

This entry has been a long time in coming, as I simply couldn't find a kind way to write about what I have come to learn about the pinky finger as well as the pinky fingernail in China. Now, however, I believe I can write in such a way that the average person will become simultaneously disgusted and intrigued. For the past three-and-a-half years, I have noticed that most of the men in China have exceedingly long pinky fingernails. While all of the other nails are neatly trimmed, the pinky nail, especially on the hands of most taxi drivers, is long enough that it has begun the slight curvature that takes place with nails that have grown long. On multiple occasions, I have witnessed the pinky fingernail inserted into the nose, followed by unabashed digging. It is as if the pinky had been specifically designated for the unseemly task of clearing the nose of debris. In a 2008 journal entry, I found where I had asked Jane (her name has been changed for protection) if the fingernail on the smallest finger had been given special privileges in China. She replied with this literal translation: "The pinky fingernail is really dirt. Most people kept their hand clean, but this fingernail use for other things. I don't like. If I see man with this, I don't want touch money from him in taxi. I know why he have this. Someone told me in India they have same idea for right and left hand. One hand is for clean and one is for dirty." Jane's words left me feeling as though I should never touch what the pinky fingernails of this country had previously touched. However, it was nice to know that the rest of the fingers were trying to be kept free from such things. In the midst of what we may consider dirty, they may actually be attempting to be sanitary.

In a second journal entry from later in 2008, Alex (again, the name has been changed) told me that fingernails are status symbols. His interpretation had everything to do with career and economic status. He said, "If you have long nails, this means you are not a farmer, working in the fields. If you can have long nails, you must have an office job or some other good job." To this, I replied, "Yes, but I have also seen taxi drivers with long nails. Are they, in fact, a part of the upper class in China?" Alex promptly responded, "They want people to think they are when they're not on the job." Alex's fingernails were neither long nor short. They were of normal length. I asked him about his fingernails, and he politely responded, "Now, Ruth, you know by now that you can't include everyone in a generalization . . . just most. I am different . . . not among the norm here. I have been exposed to many different cultures," to which I replied, "Yes, that is true, but is it a fair generalization to say that in China, most men who have long nails and/or long pinky fingernails are either using them for their noses or to imply that they are in positioned in the upper class?" He sat and pondered. We talked, and after we discussed many other subjects, he returned to my question and said, "Yes, I think it is a fair generalization." "What is?" I asked. "The finger in the nose as normal and accepted here or as a status symbol?" "Yes," he replied. "Of course, there are always exceptions, but let me ask you—what would you say are some generalizations that come with being an American?"

This is a fantastic question. What *does* that mean? Is it a good or bad thing? What would most people say about an American, a Filipino, an Israeli, a German, a . . . a . . . a . . . ? What do most people say or think about your nationality, your culture? Do you fit into the mold that has been set by society? Are you just as the generalities claim? Would you say that the generalities are true? These are all things with which we should grapple. How do we fit into our society? Do we allow ourselves to be controlled by stereotypes, or are we pioneers of personality and perseverance?

Shenzhen is quite different from the rest of China. With its proximity to Hong Kong, this city is not completely Chinese, and certainly the expatriate community is a haven from the real world of cultural veracities. How could I begin to assume that what we are experiencing in this developing area is anywhere near the norm in other inland provinces or rural China? The norm is what is accepted in an area, and the area of China is massive. To identify and simplify the culture of a small, European country or one of the United States would be dangerously haphazard and dim-witted—so to claim this with China, a land with many ethnic groups and identities would be just as assumptive. What assumptions do we make? How have we come to these postulations? Have we based them on experience or hearsay? I would challenge you to consider the means by which you develop an understanding of culture and to reflect on the implications you discover.

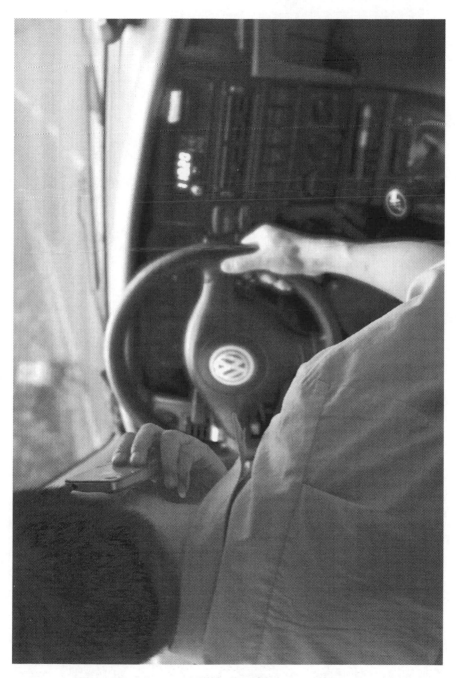

Pinky Nail

Part II

Life in China

The Language

Why is it that checking the mailbox and finding a letter feels differently than opening an inbox with emails? Is it knowing that time was spent looking up the address or addressing the envelope? Is it the sharp creases that were so carefully formed or the care with which the envelope was sealed? Is it the fact that someone purchased a stamp that would enable the letter to reach your threshold, possibly miles from its origin? Or, is it simply the excitement of finding something unexpected and heartwarming? For whatever reason, a letter is unique, inviting, and compelling. What would you do if you were unable to read the letters or even the advertisements in your mailbox?

In a land where, for centuries, characters and pictures have been used to communicate, a romanized alphabet from A to Z is foreign and still unfamiliar to the older Chinese generation. It wasn't until the late 1950s that Pinyin (the romanization of Chinese characters) was adopted. Although romanized, there are still numerous letters from the English alphabet that are nonexistent in Pinyin, and characters remain the primary means of written communication. Over time, the characters have changed from clear images of scenes that depict a story to more streamlined pictographs that have lost much of their original shapes. This simple yet intriguing aspect of the Chinese culture is one of the foundational differences between the East and the West.

To a visitor, the characters and symbols can be quite daunting. Even the tonal, spoken language itself is quite different from the Latin-derived linguistics and intonation of the West—the tones themselves are unfamiliar and abnormal. Yet, what is normal? For Chinese people, the absence of tones is unfamiliar and abnormal. In the Chinese language, there are four tones. This means, for example, that there are four different ways to say a word as well as four different meanings for that word. Intonation is vital. Take, for instance, the Chinese word "si." In the *fourth* tone, "si" means four, yet if spoken in the *first* tone, "si" means die. Interestingly, for this very reason, many buildings do not have a fourth floor.

So, whose language evolved first? Does the fact it was developed first make it somehow superior or entitling? Of course, one could conclude that superiority is far from a key issue. It is merely a difference in history and the evolution of language that brings these differences to the modern table. With brushstrokes and combinations of characters, the Chinese language unfolds. If one character stands alone, it may represent a word; however, combined with other characters it may have an entirely different meaning. For someone in the West, without Pinyin, nothing is familiar. From this, the most interesting feelings have evolved. For many postmodern artists, Chinese characters and brush strokes resurfaced and became the theme of their work. The complete impact of Mandarin has yet to be seen or felt.

Regardless of the future, submerged in a land of an unknown language, people often become uneasy and possibly condescending. Sometimes, it is a coping mechanism, while at other times it is simply defensive justification stemming from insecurity. At what point is insecurity justifiable?

Communication is at the heart of both introverted and extroverted people. Regardless of personality, communicating has molded us into who we are as well as what we will be. Whether verbal or nonverbal, each day is full of expressions and transpirations. We learn by listening, reading, and viewing; the world of communication inspires us to grow and change. Therefore, if unable to grasp the meaning of written or spoken languages, we become uncomfortable and frustrated. For many expatriates in China, it is only through nonverbal communication—charades, hand gestures, and pointing—that information is gathered. As one can imagine, however, misunderstandings surface. Chinese people are emphatic. Their expressions and actions appear loud and, at times, boisterous. They are animated, insistent, and determined to "save face." In this, their actions can be misunderstood for anger. On the contrary, they are simply expressing their opinions with gusto. In the West, gusto is usually associated with passion, and passionate people are frequently written off as extremists. Is this how we view the Chinese, then? Have we somehow become the opposite of an extremist . . . a pacifist, accepting of that which is truly questionable? Is everyone right? Is nothing considered wrong? What are we saying through our actions?

One place a Westerner might feel most alienated is along a street where the storefronts are scattered with characters and symbols. Another, more personal place might be at the mailbox. The excitement of receiving a letter in China may be dashed by the realization that the letter cannot be read. An advertisement may offer outstanding sale opportunities, yet the product is unknown to the reader. In the hands of a foreigner, it is quite possible that he or she may not differentiate between the water bill and the latest television programming publication. These are things that contribute to the shape of a foreign experience.

May 8, 2008 — The chopsticks are good for something.

I check our apartment mailbox every day. I get so excited about descending twenty-two floors and checking our tiny, black box. I find myself hoping that it will contain a letter, stamped with the *par avion* emblem. Even if I receive an advertisement for hand soap or a menu with pictures of indescribable dishes, I find an odd, yet exhilarating rush of energy surge through my entire body. I have no idea what is written on these advertisements or what the characters mean; yet I am surprisingly happy to receive this indecipherable piece of paper.

Today, I realized that my mailbox was locked, and I do not have a key. When I explained to the management (in English) that I didn't have a key, they responded (in Chinese) that someone must have put a new lock on the box, and "no can fix you problem." This is China. At times, I have seen mail delivered haphazardly, packages precariously perched on top of the mailbox or letters only halfway inside the opening, without any concern as to who might want to take the letters and/or packages therein. Therefore, I have no idea why someone, just since yesterday afternoon, has decided to lock my mailbox.

In China, the concept of privacy is ambiguous and quite subjective. With over a billion people, privacy is uncommon—more of a luxury. Many people have never been afforded the gift of privacy; but then again, most would not recognize it as a gift. It is culturally normal to be surrounded by hundreds of people. On the contrary, most Western people feel uncomfortable in a crowd. I diverge, but I will write more on this soon.

I trudged back to the mailboxes, peeking through the tiny slit to see if I could make out a silhouette or two. Yes, the box contained at least two envelopes, one of which I was sure was something I had been waiting for. I was suddenly consumed with the need to open that box and get my mail.

What would you do? If resourceful, you find a coat hanger or perhaps a file to coax the lock to open. In fact, I found myself returning to the elevator and ascending the same, familiar twenty-two floors to find something that might allow me to retrieve my coveted letters.

I then spent fifty-five minutes using a pair of chopsticks to try to pluck the letters through the tiny slot in our mailbox. I placed one of the chopsticks in my right hand and the other in my left. Sliding both between the black space, I tried to move the sticks together, as if conducting an orchestra. Every time I heard someone coming, I would quickly retrieve the chopsticks, hoping that the person coming would not think I was ridiculous for attempting such a feat. Twice, I almost succeeded in pulling the letter to the top of the box, only to watch it slip away as I let go of one chopstick to grab the letter.

Then, the worst happened, I dropped one of the chopsticks into the black abyss. What was I to do? How would I get my mail now? Would the chopstick obstruct proper delivery of additional letters (the majority of which I won't be able to read) and further impede my ability to read and understand something familiar?

Why is it that we are as drawn to a personal, handwritten letter as we might be to money? We are drawn to familiar communication and the secrets that lie within sealed letters. We yearn for familiarity and comfort. In these ways, cross-cultural humanity is the same. The mailbox to which we walk brings more than a letter; it brings hope. Why, filled with letters written in a foreign language, might the same mailbox conjure fear? The answer: it puts the receiver into the category of being an "other"—often a place of isolation and personal reflection.

Yes, the people in China also experience communication apprehension. As you will read in the following anecdote, a Shenzhen taxi driver openly explains his anxiety:

March 18, 2009— "Please, don't speak to me."

If I see a foreigner walking toward my taxi, my heart beats fast, and my palms begin to sweat. I don't know what to do. I don't know English. I speak two words: "hello" and "thank you." Sometimes they laugh when I say, "thank you." I do not know why. I know that, usually, they will either hand me a piece of paper with the Chinese address scribbled on it, probably written by a bilingual friend, or they will attempt to speak English. Often, they expect me to speak their language, but I have never needed English. I don't know what to say. Sometimes, they try to speak my language. Often, it seems that they think speaking loudly will make it easier for me to understand. It is not that I can't hear them; it's just that I can't understand them. Most of the time, when they try to speak, it is unclear and frustrating. I do not know what they are saying, and their accents are strong. I want to understand them, but they confuse the tones. In China, we have four tones, which means that one word may have many meanings. Most of the time, I spend the first five minutes trying to understand where they want to go. Don't they know that they are in my country? Can't they try to learn the language? For me, Chinese characters are easy to understand. I am used to the pictures that tell a story. Their letters don't tell me any stories.

How does your language shape the way you view your environment? Do you think about the feelings of others? Do you stop to think about how your language and other languages are related? Do you take your language for granted? Can you easily read the advertisements that reach your box? If you chose to, could you freely talk with the people next to you? Can you understand what is on the shelves in the grocery store? Have you ever been in a group where you were the only one who could not understand the language? Have you ever been the only one in the room who couldn't speak more than one language?

Can you easily read the directions on your washing machine?

March 14, 2008 — Wash, rinse, flood cycle.

How in the world am I supposed to wash my clothes when I don't even know what the hieroglyphics on my washing machine mean? Today, I flooded the entire area around the washing machine. Last week, the people from my husband's office came to label each Chinese-written button, but something was lost in the translation, and I proceeded to soak the mat as well as the box that held our recently purchased microwave. This is frustrating. I simply want to be able to read and understand the characters . . . while wearing clean clothes, of course. I won't journal long today, as I must mop up the water before it begins to mold in this humidity. And then I have to try again to figure out this machine.

April 12, 2008 — Is it because I can't speak?

I had the strangest dream last night! I was walking toward a bus stop, and I started salivating. I could *not* stop, and I began to drool. I pulled tissues from my handbag to control the fluid, but I was salivating so profusely that I placed the entire wad of tissues in my mouth as though it were gauze in a dental office — in fact, as I stuffed them in, that's what they became. I had chipmunk cheeks and a fellow English-speaking expat ran up to me, asking if I was okay. When I tried to explain, I couldn't because my cheeks were so full of gauze. The man picked me up and placed me in a taxi. The next thing I knew, I was in a hospital with rows and rows of people who also had chipmunk cheeks. They were all lying in bed with balls of gauze in their mouths. A doctor came and explained that I was part of an epidemic that had just erupted, and he quickly asked: "Have you had noodles today?" I nodded with a yes because I couldn't speak, and no one would remove the gauze. He went on to explain that I would salivate profusely for the next seven days before they could give me the vaccine. The doctor also explained that my husband, John, was the one who had gone to get the vaccine, which was in Indonesia. What a nightmare! What does this mean? Am I so bothered by the language barrier and the inability to communicate that I have begun to have absurd dreams? What does isolation instigate?

police sign

The next time you order Chinese takeout and reach for your chopsticks, chuckle at these anecdotes. Furthermore, the next time you open your mailbox, read an advertisement in your native language, find the correct cycle on your washing machine, or ask for directions, contemplate the ease with which you can communicate and relay your thoughts. Contemplate the importance of accepting and embracing your native language as well as respecting the languages of those you meet. Can we learn to respect unfamiliarity? If we want harmony, it is essential.

The Beauty

For centuries, men and women have enjoyed the benefits of spa treatments and ultimate relaxation. From the earliest infamous Roman baths to the fish spa—where fish nibble off dead skin from the feet—spa services have become something to which many people gravitate for de-stressing. This temporary relief is usually followed in a week by the all-too-common exclamation, "I need a day at the spa." What is it that we enjoy most about being pampered? Is it the opportunity to lie flat for a while? Is it that we can close our eyes and listen to tranquil music? Is it that we can feel water bubbling between our toes, somehow "taking us away from it all?" Is it simply that we can rely on someone else to rub the aches of walking, lifting, pulling, sitting, etc.? Whatever the case, spas have continued to offer multiple options for the "pamperee." In China, the spas are full of packages for dealing with every imaginable ache, pain, or beauty treatment. On almost every corner, a fully staffed spa can be found.

December 27, 2007—"Lie down on this bed; I will wash your hair."

Keep in mind that this is my first trip to China, and I have only been here five days. On my first day, my flat iron (hair straightener) started smoking in the hotel bathroom and proceeded to blow up! Yes, on the first day, I learned that the wattage is completely different here. I no longer have a way to straighten my hair and, in this humidity, I need it. I am sure I look like Bozo the clown to these people who have straight, black hair. Two days ago, I also found myself eating fish head for Christmas dinner with some ladies from the office and now, I find I have agreed to accompany them to a popular Chinese hair salon for a hair wash. What have I done? We are riding in this taxi, and I am a bit confused about what they are trying to articulate. Apparently, I will lie down on a foam bed and the salon man will wash my hair. My head and back will be massaged, and I will feel "free from life." I am not sure if they want me to go to the salon because my hair is frizzy and they think I need it, or because this is truly going to be an unforgettable experience . . . in more ways than one. All I can picture is water being poured on my head and the bed becoming a royal mess of shampoo and conditioner. I hope I haven't made a big mistake.

(at the salon)

We've come into the salon, and there are at least twenty male stylists running around in black shirts and tight, black trousers with trendy-looking belts. They all have spiky hairdos. As Sanny stands at the reception desk and explains the service we are requesting, I sit on this black sofa to write about what I see. Someone just came to ask me, *"Ni yo meiyo shui?"* I have no idea what that means, but Sanny is quick to ask, "Do you want some water?" They run off and bring back a small, paper cup of warm water. The man who brought it to me acts as though he may have never seen a foreign person before. I am not in a highly-traveled expat area. Maybe I am the first foreign person he has ever seen. He motions for my handbag and Sanny says, "it's okay." I hand the bag to him and wait to see what is next. He brings back a key which belongs to my locker. I now have a locker, and my handbag is in the locker. Sanny explains that I can keep my things in there until we are done.

hand massage

The place is clean and the floors show no sign of hair, but that may be because there are three or four young ladies who are walking around with brooms. I think their only job may be to sweep the floor—I guess, with a population this size, jobs must be created. However, I can't imagine sweeping the floor for hours on end. I also notice that there are different outfits for each job. It seems that the guys in all black are the stylists, while the people who are wearing white and black apply color. I wonder where the hair-washing beds are located. I feel a bit uneasy. I can tell that I don't really fit here, and I definitely can't decipher what is being said, let alone whispered, as I sit here and take in the stares.

* * *

Time has passed since this morning's hair washing, and now I can recount the entire experience. What a memorable, completely unforgettable day! I have never experienced anything like this in my entire life! A petite Chinese woman guided me into a small robing room where she asked me to put on a cape. As I awkwardly handed my paper cup to her, she assisted me with the cape and escorted me into a room with two rows of beds. To be honest, they looked like black coffins with vinyl encasings. At the end of each coffin—I mean, bed—were basins with drains and a pedestal in the center which was the same height as the bed. The pedestals were flat and wide. I could see a few customers who were already lying down, backs to the beds, with their heads resting on the pedestals above the basins. Their hair dangled down into the washbasin, and they all appeared to be completely at ease. I was guided to the third bed, and I was surprised to find that the vinyl lining was softer than I expected. I sat down and waited for instructions. Then a man arrived and motioned for me to lie down on my back with my head over the basin. I leaned back and realized that he was now sitting on a stool, right above my head and the area where my hair rested. From my vantage point, he was upside down, and his hands were already reaching for the water.

He began by drenching my hair. The first thing I realized was that my neck was completely relaxed. It wasn't like the places at home where you are expected to lean back in an extremely uncomfortable chair with your neck at a ninety-degree angle on a hard, ceramic bowl. Although I have always been completely satisfied with the American hairdresser I use, I can only imagine the increase in satisfaction if they had these basin-beds! I was completely comfortable and relaxed. He began to massage my forehead, slowly working down toward my temples and then running his hands gently through my wet hair, massaging the scalp in a slow, circular pattern. After approximately ten minutes, he lathered the shampoo and began to wash my hair. He washed my hair for at least five minutes and then rinsed with the same process as before. The best part was yet to come. After he put the conditioner in my hair, he spent twenty minutes massaging my scalp and neck. He often pulled my head toward where he was sitting, away from my feet in an upward and gentle draw. With the conditioner still in my hair, he used his palms and fingers to press and release along the base of my skull, following the curve of my head toward the top of my cranium. It was so different from a hair-washing back home.

Following the final rinse, he then massaged my back. Finally, the experience concluded, and I was sad that it had come to an end. What I had thought would be a simple, five-minute wash-and-go had turned into a forty-five minute hair wash with massage. I felt like a new person, indeed, "free from life."

I replaced the cape and walked out to the reception area where Sanny was waiting for me. I know she could tell by my expression that I had thoroughly enjoyed this outing. I am touched by her genuine interest in my happiness. She wants me to have many wonderful moments while here, and although much of what I have witnessed and/or experienced hasn't been what I consider to be typically comforting, I can see that this is normal life in China. She is certainly trying to make me feel more at home. How do I make people feel when they come to visit me? Where would I take them? Do I have their interests at heart? Do I want them to be happy; do I consider their needs?

How often do we forget to accommodate our guests? Do we think that the rest of the world should conform to our standard way of life? If so, why do we feel that way? How do we justify those feelings?

There are many spa options in China. One of the most interesting aspects of spas in China is, much like a gym in the States, a person can purchase a membership. The membership works a little differently, though, than most gym memberships. For instance, a person might purchase a membership card for 1,000 yuan. Each time the person visits the spa, the amount of the service is deducted from the original membership fee, much like a debit system. The benefit of having the card as opposed to paying per visit is that, upon presenting the card, the customer receives a twenty percent discount for each service. Therefore, if a facial is listed at 100 yuan, the customer pays 80 yuan and is left with 920 yuan on the membership card. Packages allow people to specifically choose the service they are seeking. For many, ear candling has become a popular add-on. In this process, wax is literally burned from the ear. A tube is inserted into the ear and a flame is lit at the opposite end of the tube. As the flame burns, it pulls wax from the ear, leaving it free from dirt and build-up. Although many may curl their noses at the idea, it may be an innocuous way to rid the ear of unnecessary wax, rather than pushing the excess further into the ear canal.

In China, taking care of oneself might also include skin-whitening treatments. Interestingly, the fascination with Western appearance is primarily a result of advertisements. Typically, the fashion industry uses Western models. Therefore, it is not hard to deduce that multiple modeling agencies target the expatriate areas, and several families have permitted their children to model for major Chinese brands.

September 11, 2011—How tall is she?

At times, the obsession is a bit overwhelming and disturbing. For three months now, I haven't been out without being approached at least—at least!—once a week by modeling agents, asking if Claire would be willing to model. I have nothing against modeling, but it is as though we are targeted. Yesterday, I received a phone call from someone that I didn't know. The following was our conversation:

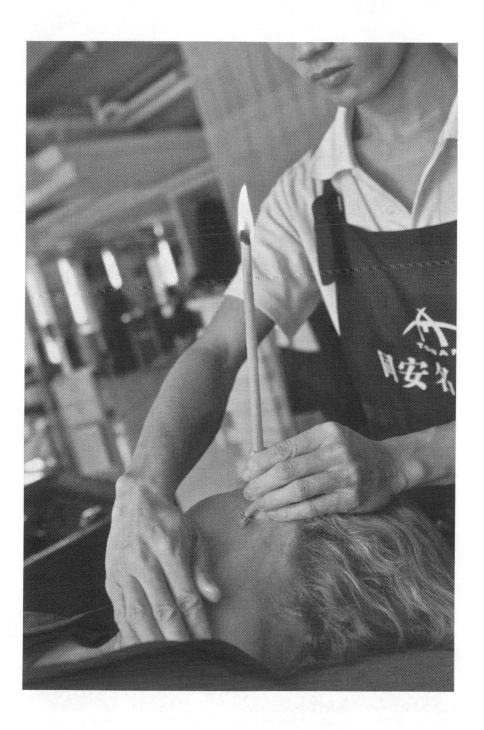

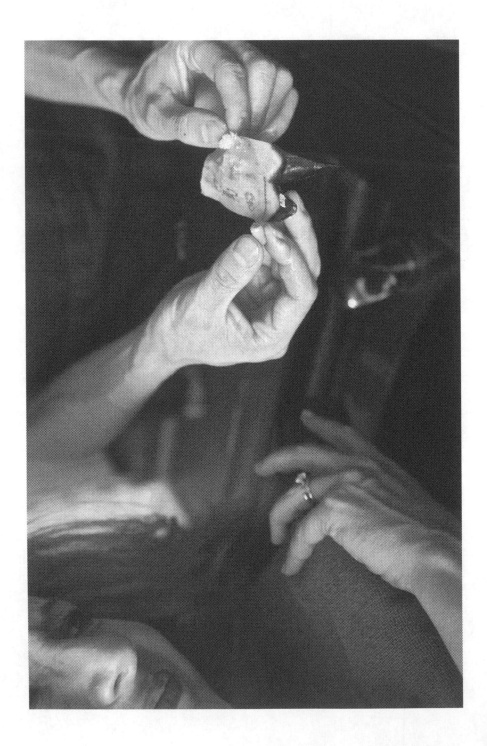

Sue: "Hello. How tall is she?"

Me: "How tall is who?"

Sue: "Your daughter."

Me: "Who is this?"

Sue: "This is Sue, and I am calling about your daughter. Would she like to be a model?"

Me: "Please hold for a moment, let me ask her . . . (Claire, would you like to be a model?) . . . no, I am sorry."

Sue: "Okay, well, maybe I will call you next week to see if you are available."

Me: "No, but thank you."

Sue: "Okay, talk to you next week."

There are also times that I watch as Chinese people flock to where a Western person is standing, simply because they want to see what he/she is doing and, possibly, be a part of it. Many nationals assume that a foreigner is wealthy. Therefore, if a foreigner is interested in something, it must be good. The connections and assumptions are based merely on what they have been told, what they see, and superficial correlations between wealth and happiness. On the other hand, many Chinese people are becoming extremely wealthy themselves and have begun to consider their own strength and status. I am sure the upcoming years will be full of interesting paradigm shifts.

I don't know who coined the idiom, "beauty is in the eye of the beholder." However, this might be the best way to describe the indescribable, especially when beauty is concerned.

quest for curly hair

The Tea

In China, what is the equivalent of coffee in Europe or America? The answer is simple: tea. As common as it is to sit around a Western table, cup of coffee in hand, chatting about world events, Chinese hands are graced with tea. A familiar and welcomed tradition in most of the coastal provinces such as Guangdong and Fujian, tea is rich in history. Family and friends often come together over tea, discussing current events and playing Mahjong or listening to traditional music. Tea can be found in cups or in bottles. It is as common as water or sports drinks are at a local sports field.

April 3, 2008 — Tea at my house, anyone?

I have never, in my entire life, seen as much tea as I saw today. Karen (a Chinese friend of mine) asked me if I wanted to go to a traditional teahouse after lunch. Imagining teahouses in America, I experienced a momentary sense of warmth. Based on my limited exposure and cultural influences, I pictured ladies in hats, sitting at tables with clean, white or pastel-colored table linens. I visualized the menu with lengthy lists of petit fours, sandwiches, pastries, and delectable teas with fancy names. I imagined the little tea bags and strainers used to diffuse the strength and flavor of the tea. I pictured small spoons with delicate designs as well as beautiful china to adorn each table. I found myself uniquely excited about the adventure and decided that I would enjoy my first experience in a traditional Chinese teahouse.

Little did I know that the teahouse would look nothing like I imagined. The small shop was dark and lined with glass display cases. The shelves, which held multiple tea tins and beautifully packaged box sets, were made of dark wood, and a man in the corner was dangling a cigarette from slightly parted lips. The smell of cigarette smoke and tea permeated the air. Within a few minutes, he was asked to retrieve some tea from the top shelf, so he freed his hands and reached for a red can of tea. The customer read the label, seemingly pleased with her selection. A long table, large decorative tiles adorning the top, was centered in the shop, and four wooden trays held beautiful teapots with small, matching ceramic teacups. The teacups didn't have handles; they were simple, yet beautiful. The man said something loudly in Mandarin, and a petite lady emerged from a doorway in the back of the shop.

Karen and I were escorted to the table. "*Qing zuo* (Please, sit)," said the lady. We sat down, and an amazing display unfolded. Karen selected the tea. There were no tea bags and no strainers. There were no small spoons . . . no white linens . . . no hats. First, the lady heated the water. I was told that the temperature must be exactly nineteen degrees Celsius, and that it was important that tea be steeped in this way, as to protect the flavor and nutritional value of the tea. There were two rounds of pouring. The first round was discarded. I watched as she poured tea from the teapot (which had a built-in strainer). The tea slid perfectly down the insides of the cup, never splashing or sloshing a single drop, and the ease with which she moved from one cup to another and back to the pot indicated years of practice. After pouring each cup, she returned to take the tea and discard it. I was confused. Why had she poured tea and immediately discarded it? Then, I was told that there are two beliefs regarding this tradition: some believe that the first round is to "wash" the tea, while others believe that the first round is to release the strongest tea. "Time is the most important part," Karen translated. "If the tea is kept too long or not long enough, it ruins the flavor. If the temperature isn't exactly nineteen degrees, the tea will lose its maximum benefit." I have never looked at tea with such detail. My ways seem haphazard and careless. After today, I wonder if my tea would taste repulsive to the people of China. Had I ruined every cup of tea I had ever attempted to prepare? Were their "other" ways as strange as my own "other" ways? At this time, I perceive that I, as well as my entire culture, may be lacking information about the art of serving tea.

After the second round of tea was poured, I was told to sip it. It was so different—bitter, yet strong and refreshing. No sugar was offered, and milk had no place at our table. There were no pastries or sandwiches to change the flavor, and it was somehow pure and complete without the extras. "Food interrupts," Karen interpreted. I had never thought of food as interrupting anything! This is definitely something I must consider. Does my food interrupt and somehow ruin a good drink?

Although this tea was satiating, Karen also explained that other teas are designed to accompany specific Chinese food types. I suppose this could be equated to the way wine accompanies and enhances food (red wine to red meat, white wine to fish or chicken, beer to fried foods, etc.). At this point, I don't think I am ready to understand how the teas are matched to various foods. There were far too many teas in this teahouse for me to begin.

Although the experience was far different from home, I find myself reflecting on the beauty within this tea ceremony. There is something special about the way in which tea is served here. I can't define it. It's a bit mysterious, as though the lady pouring the tea knows something that a foreigner, like me, would never be able to understand or appreciate. I felt somewhat inferior—not in a condescending sort of way, but I knew she was the expert in the room. When do we feel as though we are the experts? Do we only feel this way in our own, familiar environments? Is it good to ever feel as though we have reached the expert level? I would venture to say that there are times when we should remember that other cultures can teach us much!

The multiple health benefits of drinking tea have long been a part of the Chinese belief system. Although a huge part of the traditional culture, the reasons for drinking tea go far beyond mere custom. In China, drinking hot liquids is thought to be good for circulation. The idea of putting ice in a drink is foreign and considered bad for the body. Chinese people believe that cold drinks, as well as cold food, will slow down the rate of digestion. Most Chinese food contains various types of oil; the people trust that tea assists the stomach in digesting and protecting the body from possibly harmful effects.

February 1, 2009—Some like it hot; some like it cold.

I scalded the top of my mouth, again, today! I don't know why I haven't become accustomed to the cup of boiling water that is commonly served in the restaurants. Is it so embedded in my Western upbringing that cold, or at least room temperature, water will be in the glass? Whatever the reason, I can't seem to remember that hot water is preferred. Yes, back home, hot is associated with coffee and tea. A simple glass of water is never served hot. I wonder if people in America once enjoyed simple, hot water? Where did the change begin? When did we start putting ice in our drinks and wanting our fluids to be cold? Is it true that cold drinks are less conducive to our natural body temperatures, therefore affecting digestion? Is that part of the reason that so many Americans are obese? Maybe, just maybe, I should consider drinking hot water or green tea. Oh, if only I could keep the tea leaves from slipping into my mouth. (Last week, William told me I put too many tea leaves in the cup—I used enough for ten cups of tea—oops! I have to learn.) There are no tea bags here, just tea leaves or flower petals and stems floating around in the water. How do they keep the tiny pieces from slipping down the throat? Do they often swallow them? Is there an art to drinking it, just as there is to pouring it? Yet, again, I have much to learn. Don't we all?

I won't write much more this evening, as four Chinese women just exited our apartment. They had an "intervention" for me. One of the ladies that works in the office saw me eating an ice cream cone. Cold items are typically frowned upon; however, when you are pregnant, it is without a doubt, taboo! I won't elaborate on all of the "pregnancy rules" that I was given tonight, but suffice it to say that I shouldn't be eating ice cream. It is "bad for your baby."

October 21, 2010—Hop back on.

Today, I asked for a cup of hot water! What is happening? Is this an example of saturation? Will I ever fit in to a particular culture again? Is it like riding a bike? Can I hop back on without missing a beat? I don't even know what is popular in the States right now. Every time I go home, I hear someone say, "Have you seen that commercial about ____; isn't it hilarious?" Have I become somehow obsolete? I'll sit and think now . . . .

Hospitality is demonstrated in a variety of cultural ways. Often, at the lack of knowing the customs, we find ourselves in an uncomfortable situation. In some European countries, it is impolite to visit a home without bringing a small token of appreciation (flowers, food, etc.). In America, it is polite to offer guests something to drink. For Filipinos, it is important to provide both food and drink. When a baby is born in Belgium, it is customary for visitors to the hospital or home to receive a small gift. For the people of China, it is customary to provide green or red tea in the home. For very special occasions and sometimes as gifts, Puer (black tea—the most prestigious in China) is purchased. Even amid business meetings, economic sectors, and procurement teams who are visiting factories, tea has a prominent place, deeply embedded in the culture.

. . . perfectly down the insides of the cup, never splashing or sloshing a single drop, and the ease with which she moved from one cup to another and back to the pot indicated years of practice.

There was, and still is, something beautiful in this . . . never to be forgotten.

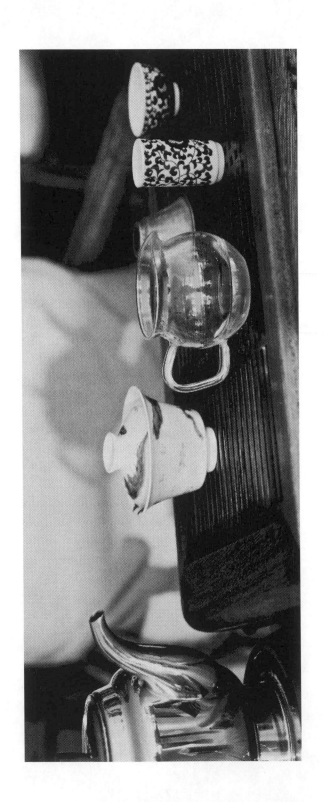

The Food

One of the first things people usually ask me is, "Do you like the food in China?" Food—an enjoyable topic, and one that speaks volumes about personal backgrounds, preferences, and ethnicity. If someone hears "croissant," they usually think of French pastries and the delectable cuisine in France. If "hamburgers" are mentioned, an instant association with America is made. In the same way, "dumplings" have a unique relationship with Asian cuisine. When various countries are mentioned, a wide range of food comes to mind.

It may be easy to presume that staple foods are universal, yet this couldn't be further from the truth. Staple foods in America consist of milk, butter, cheese, grains, and (some would say) peanut butter. In France, bread adorns every kitchen counter. In Mexico, standard items on the grocery list are onions, cornmeal, and beans. Belgium is known for its exquisite chocolate, even though it's not a staple food. New Zealand boasts some of the best dairy products in the world. And China? Generally speaking, Chinese cupboards contain the following staple foods: rice, garlic, oil, eggs, and noodles. Of course, there are a variety of meats and vegetables that are added to the shelves, but these items are essential for authentic Chinese cuisine. Back to the original question: "Do you like the food in China?" This is like asking if I like the food in America. As anywhere, there are things that I like and things that I don't like.

Often, it is not the food itself that conjures uneasiness, but the unfamiliarity of an entree. When a new, unidentifiable dish has been served, young children often ask their parents, "What is this?" Usually, this question is followed by hesitation and coaxing. If we don't know what has been served and we can't classify it, we probably won't try it. More often than not, it is my own naivete that has kept me from exploring more Chinese cuisine.

December 25, 2007 — The eyeball is yours . . .
Merry Christmas!

I cried tonight! It is Christmas, and I am sitting in our small studio apartment in the heart of Shenzhen. The glow of the lights from surrounding skyscrapers is cascading across my paper. As I write, I can hear the water rushing through the pipes behind me as my husband takes a shower. Outside, I can hear the brakes of buses screeching between each stop, and the train has just passed on its 9:00 p.m. journey to Guangzhou. I turn on the television, hoping to see something familiar—a Christmas tree or a familiar Christmas movie—but nothing remotely associated to Christmas could be found. I imagine that my family is just beginning their day in America. I imagine my mother putting the turkey in the oven and my brothers sitting on the staircase for the annual Christmas morning picture, and I am sure my dad is saying, "Thank you, Saaaanta, wherever you are." I miss them.

At least three times this morning, the same commercial (in Mandarin) has played, and I think I may be able to decipher what they are advertising, but now I just want to turn it off and recoil into a world of things that are familiar. If I look out the window, I see signs that are full of messages that I cannot read, and I have begun to wonder if I will ever fit in here. I suppose I am feeling a bit negative tonight, yet I don't want my husband to know that I am sad, as I know this is an exciting move for him. I am sure these are natural feelings; it is only through challenging times that we grow, learn new things, and appreciate the good things we have.

I could be negative about the following story, but I will tell it lightheartedly and, maybe one day, I will look back at this story and chuckle.

We went to lunch with Pam and Tom today. They are from two different provinces in China. Although each province has a unique taste, these two knew about a restaurant that combined many Chinese flavors and, knowing that today was Christmas, they asked us if we would like to have Christmas dinner together at a great Chinese restaurant. Excitedly, we agreed! When we reached the restaurant, the entire menu was in characters, so we decided it would be best to encourage Pam and Tom to order. Occasionally, they would ask us if we liked certain things: "Chicken? Broccoli? Spicy Noodle?"

The table was round with a lazy susan in the middle. After ordering, the waitress brought a bowl of peanuts as well as some cucumber sticks in soy sauce with small, red peppers. I watched as Pam and Tom reached for their chopsticks and clasped a peanut between the ends of the slippery, black sticks. They made it look so easy. I reached for my chopsticks, receiving instructions on how to hold the two daggers. After getting my hands adjusted and feeling confident that I could grab a peanut, I reached forward to snag one. After two minutes, I lost feeling in my hands. I was gripping the chopsticks too hard, and I could feel my ring finger aching with what felt like arthritis pains. It took me almost five minutes amid multiple drops, to finally get one, lousy oily peanut; those peanuts were slippery, but I finally managed to keep it lodged between the chopsticks long enough to reach my mouth. In starvation, I chewed with triumph. The cucumber sticks were easier to grasp; however, with their rectangular shape, I didn't know what to do when it was within an inch of my mouth. The cucumber was vertical, and my mouth is horizontal, so I cocked my head to one side, feeling utterly ridiculous and scooped my mouth under the cucumber, like a baby bird accepting a worm from its mother.

The meal continued, with everything from spicy beef to shark-fin soup. Then came the climatic moment. A fish was delivered to the lazy susan, and the entire fish, nose to fins, was lying on our Christmas-day table. Pam readjusted her legs under the table and sat up a little straighter. I looked over at her, and she appeared to be contemplating the moment. She was staring at the fish and then spoke to Tom in Mandarin. After they held a short, indecipherable, conversation, Pam said, "John, we like you to be the one who have fish eye today to honor first Christmas in Shenzhen." John's eyes looked directly into the fish's, and I could only think to myself, "Please, do not eat the eye, or all I will be able to think about is how you swallowed an eyeball." He quickly and diplomatically replied, "That is most kind, but we should be honoring you, our host." After some convincing, Pam accepted the honor and devoured the fish's eyeball. I smiled at her, yet my brain was not there. It was miles away, wondering if my mother's Christmas turkey still had an eye when it was pulled from the oven, who would have been the distinguished recipient?

Now, I sit here and anxiously think about the next dinner engagement. What other things might I be asked to eat? How will I defer "special honors"? How can I—will I ever—get over the cultural crevasse that seems to be separating me, already, from them?

In China, many people believe that each part of an animal's body is extremely influential and, if eaten, has a positive correlation or impact on that particular human organ. For example, eating eyeballs is considered extremely beneficial for the health of your eyes, and eating brain relieves migraines and helps reduce or alleviate many long-term medical ailments relating to the brain. While attending a recent dinner with a group of international businessmen in China (four years after my initial introduction to fish eyes), the visiting American was given the opportunity to eat the eyeball. Upon his deference, I found an opportunity to ask questions regarding the believed benefits of eating those various parts of the animal which we do not customarily consume. I asked the man who was sitting opposite me, "What, specifically, is to be gained from eating the eyeball of a fish?" His most honest reply included the following line: "the nutrients that are found in an eyeball will go to your eyeballs, just like the vitamins in a carrot add to those particular vitamins that are already in the body." It sounded logical. For many in China, this philosophy still holds true today. This might explain why I found braised pig intestines on a popular

Chinese restaurant's menu. Yes, if a person has irritable bowels, eating intestines might help.

February 10, 2009—No, thank you, no braised pig intestines today. Umm, maybe next time?

I am pregnant. The first three months were full of nausea; yet I am happy to report that it has finally subsided! However, today was an exception. I think this was probably the first recurrence of nausea that I have had in two weeks. How can I write about this and think that someone back home would not believe me? I know that these ideas seem anomalous and, actually, far-fetched. I think the only people that can fully understand and recognize that these anecdotes are real as well as appreciate the impact they have on our life experiences are those expatriates that are here with me. My hat goes off to those who are experiencing the same things. Yes, on the menu, was listed: "braised pig intestines." Below, I recount:

I sat next to Hilary, simply staring down at the list of characters and English subtitles. The list was filled with the typical selections of various rice, noodles, vegetables, meat, and teas. However, one item caught my eye. I turned to Hilary with a flood of questions, "Is this a literal translation? What do the characters say? Can this be right?" Hilary looked at me with a bewildered expression. "Yes, Ruth, these are pig intestines that have been 'burned on top of stove.' " I think my expression was confusing to her, so I explained, "I have never seen anything like this listed on a menu." She elaborated on the benefits of eating intestines, especially if someone may have problems with "tummy aching or go to the bathroom many times."

flower shop

Can this be true? Is this something that is widely accepted? On what grounds? Did I miss a medical study on intestinal benefits? If so, it would have been helpful to know this when I was younger, dealing with insufficient levels of the lactase enzyme (by the way, one in four Chinese people are lactose intolerant . . . interesting). On the menu, I also saw ox tongue soup. I suppose if your tongue is hurting, you might want to order this as an appetizer. I sound sarcastic, but I don't know how else to react. I know that my Western exposure has severely warped my tolerance, and I find myself ashamed that I curl my nose at something that has been eaten by the Chinese people for centuries with absolutely no side effects. Generalizations . . . this book is full of them, yet they cannot be separated from our natural existence. To believe that they can be avoided is ignorant and unrealistic.

What things do we eat that they would be surprised by? Come to think of it, there is something, a mannerism that relates to the method of eating our food, which they find appalling. Despite what I think is gross, they provide plastic gloves at KFC so that they don't have to touch their chicken wings with grimy fingers. Yes, in the local Kentucky Fried Chicken fast-food chains, they provide plastic gloves. In America, I can only picture a drive-through window, where a person pulls up to the window, reaches for their wallet or into the console for spare change, passes the money to the cashier, touches the cup or bag where the others have touched the bag, puts the car in drive, and reaches down into the bag with the same filthy hand, to eat their chicken leg. Now, people in China would think *this* is revolting. Yes, despite the things that have been said about food and mannerisms, there are things that I must remember about China. The reason that people don't wear their shoes in the house is because the streets are gritty and filled with rubbish. Knowing this, the people take special precautions to keep from tracking the muck into the home. Isn't this a good example of cleanliness? Each culture has both problems and perks. If I try to focus on the perks in each culture, I will enjoy life. Why don't I do this? Why must I be reminded to stay positive? It seems much easier back home, yet I feel that this is because a certain standard is inherently embedded, and it takes years, maybe a lifetime, to identify the standard before one can begin to adequately address cultural expectations.

I wrote the following line on the back of my *fapio* (receipt): "Although I feel a bit queasy right now, I don't think I will be able to take Hilary's advice about eating braised pig intestines to make my intestines 'unqueasy'." I wonder what else I have yet to learn about food.

The selections of noodles, rice, and dumplings are endless. These three staples have been perfected and, it comes as no surprise, unique to China's cuisine. Each province in China boasts a particular style and flavor. For instance, Sichuan province is known for its spicy flare and many have heard of the Sichuan pepper. Guangdong province is known for dim sum (dumplings), and Beijing is famous for bone marrow soups. Chinese recipes rarely exclude the use of oil. In any given grocery store, oil is given the same amount of space as cereal in an American supermarket. Yes, jugs of various oils are neatly aligned and have gained a prominent place in most kitchens. Someone once asked, "does the food in China taste the same as our Chinese food in America?" The answer: a simple no. Particular seasonings, style, and methods of preparation have been altered to appease the American palate.

eating in the middle of the street

Sugar is rarely used in Chinese recipes. Ovens are almost nonexistent in Chinese homes; everything is done on the stove. Having an oven requires a special request and is usually found only in expatriate areas. Chinese entrees are quick, and the method of preparation, efficient. Many believe that the lack of sugar in the Chinese diet, along with genetics, is what allows the majority of the people to remain slim. Although this claim may hold much truth, twenty years from now, I fear that many Chinese people will face the same obesity issues that Americans are currently facing. More and more of the younger generation gravitate to the fast-food chains and local pastry shops. After recently reading that sugar is as addictive as many potent narcotics, the idea that sugar may infiltrate and permeate the Chinese bloodstream leaves sugar companies with potentially expanding markets.

Despite these possibilities, it would be hard to believe that sugar might win against China's bone-in soup.

> *April 23, 2008—Just take your straw, insert it into the bone shaft, and suck up the soup.*

This afternoon, I had the best soup I have ever tasted in my entire life! John and I met at a place across from the office in LuoHu. Walking through the entrance, I wasn't sure if we were at a restaurant or a bank. A lady dressed in what looked like a prom dress showed us to the second floor. There were dark round tables and intricately carved wooden wall-hangings. In the middle of each table was a hole with a burner. At the tables where people were already seated, a pot had been placed on the burner, and there was steam rising from the shiny, stainless steel bowls. As the lady in the prom dress showed us to our table, I could smell something aromatic and extremely calming. The steam was somehow soothing as it drifted up from the tables. The patrons at each table spoke to each other through the vapors. I was told that we had come to have "hot pot."

We were seated, and the waitress lit our burner. She placed a pot on the flame and poured broth from an oversized kettle with an elongated spout into the big boiling pot. Within minutes, the rich broth was bubbling. Steam rose from the bowl, and I could feel myself getting hot. In Shenzhen, April feels like the beginning of summer to me. I had a sleeveless sweater on, but I don't think the fact that I didn't have sleeves made the sweater any less of a sweater. It was hot, and I had to dab my nose with the napkins. As the broth bubbled wildly, a variety of platters were brought to the table. One platter was full of mushrooms—some varieties of which I had never seen before—yet I was assured that they were mushrooms. Another platter held a display of thin meat strips, while another was filled with uncooked balls of meat. A smaller platter of spices, peppers, and vegetables was delivered to the table, and then the final platter: a large platter with four large bones, looking something like a joint with meat still affixed to the sinews surrounding the bones.

As each platter arrived, I was versed on the procedure: First, select the meat, vegetables, etc. and put them in the boiling broth. While waiting, talk with your friends, colleagues, etc. Finally, retrieve the cooked food from the broth and place it on your individual plate. Each person had a bowl of rice, and the broth could also be poured over the rice. I preferred it this way, as it allowed me to use the small, ceramic spoon rather than the chopsticks. However, even if I had used the chopsticks and placed the rice bowl to the edge of my lips and shoveled the rice in, I have learned that it is not, in the least, offensive.

fast food

restaurant

The food was so good! I enjoyed watching the food bob to the top of the pot, as if to say, "I am done now; please get me out of here." The conversation among diners continued, and the four large joints were placed into the boiling broth. After about fifteen minutes, I was given a pair of gloves. The joint was placed on my plate; it resembled an oversized rack of ribs. I was handed a straw. I immediately placed the straw in my small cup of tea, and my husband's colleague laughed at me. "What are you doing?" she exclaimed. "I don't know. What am I supposed to do with this straw?" I questioned. She picked up her straw, plunged it into the bone shaft and began sucking with all of her strength. The sound of juice, air, and lodged meat resounded in the air. It sounded much like the end of a cookies-n-cream milkshake, with remnants of the cookie coming in between loud slurps. I stared. I couldn't believe what I was seeing. She said, "This will make your bones strong! Try it!" In China, I had seen straws for many things, including straws attached to containers of yogurt in all the convenience stores, but this . . . this was quite different.

The broth had been pure and rich . . . probably the best I have ever tasted. Actually, it tasted as if it had come directly from the bones and hours upon hours of simmering. It was delectable. The meat had been deliciously succulent. The vegetables had been bright and rich with flavor. For no reason should I have thought that the bone marrow would have tasted any different, but for some reason, I just couldn't bring myself to jab the straw down in the bone. I looked directly across the table at my husband, who had placed the plastic glove on his left hand. Holding the joint with his left and taking the straw in his right, he muttered, "when in Rome . . ." I stared at him as he sucked the final parts of the marrow. He looked up and said, "Mmm, that is good; you should try it." What was holding me back? I will never know the answer to that question. My justifications include: "I am just not used to it; it is unfamiliar; nobody that I know does that." And, of course, I find myself thinking that these are all quite lame excuses for not indulging in what may have been the best thing I had ever tasted. When we hold back and listen to possible cultural biases and expectations, what do we miss out on? What regrets might we have if we continue to base everything on what is "normal" or reputable in our society?

Since that day, I have learned a lot about hot pot. Often, a pot may have a divider, which meets the needs of those who enjoy spicy food. On one side, the bland broth is provided and on the other, the spicy version. In addition, a ceramic dish with dividers is often placed in front of each individual plate with the option to add a variety of sauces, which can be combined to enhance the flavor. Many places in America have begun to adopt the idea of hot pot, and it is quite common to hear about this "new idea, where you cook at your table." However, I am not convinced that the concept is exactly the same. In China, the meat is fresh, to the point that, if seafood, it may still be alive when it is brought to the table. I vividly remember seeing shrimp in the midst of convulsions as they waited to take the "great plunge" into the boiling water. We were at a restaurant near the skating rink at The Mix C in LuoHu, and the shrimp were still alive; one of the shrimp even flopped onto the floor. In America, the idea of hot pot may not be new, but the idea of serving truly fresh seafood for you to boil in your pot may be.

In China, hot pot is another way to enjoy a family style meal. Not only is the food good, but it also gives friends and family the opportunity to sit and talk about daily events in life. It creates a fun way to involve people in the cooking process, while eliminating the time-consuming preparatory work. In America, one of the lengthiest parts of hunting is the gutting, cleaning, and curing that takes place after the animal is killed. In China, the average person has a role in this process; however, when the responsibility is alleviated, it gives the consumer a sense of freedom. As more and more grocery stores offer prepared meats, they have taken on the look of Western stores, with packaged portions and frozen options.

There are still many places throughout Asia, however, that allow you to select your animal and wait while it is prepared. One such place in Shanghai, which I thought was a pet store, awakened me to new understandings. The answer to the question that is so often posed—Do they eat dog?—is yes, in some provinces they do, but allow me to elaborate. Then ask yourself if you have the right to gasp.

Summer 2008—Daisy's wedding dog.

Tonight, John and I attended a wedding. We are in Shanghai, and I must say that I was impressed by The Bund, a famous embankment along the Huangpu River. It is full of bright lights, towering skyscrapers, and various architectural styles from its years as an international hub for trade and commerce. While standing there, I wondered how many people had traversed the same section of pavement I occupied. With millions of people dispersed over fifteen districts, Shanghai is massive and, despite its age, full of energy. I don't know in which part of Shanghai we attended the wedding; however, I know that it took us approximately thirty minutes to reach the venue from the well-known JC Mandarin Hotel. As the groom was a Frenchman and the lady Chinese, the wedding and the attendees were a blend of two cultures. As one of only five Americans, I felt as though this was an event that I would not too quickly forget. The car came to a stop in front of a uniquely European stone building. The entrance resembled the portico of a castle. I could see that this place was special and the unique design made me wonder if the building was a popular gathering place in Shanghai. Throughout the night, no one was able to answer this question, but I will remember its impact, as I haven't seen anything up until now that looked anything like this building in China.

soup bowls

your soup bowl

We walked down a meticulously groomed, grassy thoroughfare. The gardens were beautiful, and the stone walkway matched the architectural style of the immediate surroundings. Although aesthetically pleasing and unique, I couldn't help but notice four large, glass windows to my right. The first thing I noticed behind the glass was a large, golden retriever. The dog was beautiful. I stopped and looked past my reflection to the inside of the animal-filled room. Each in their own designated crates or water containers, I saw frogs, turtles, snakes, dogs, rabbits, small alligators, and birds. Shocked, I asked Sam, the man who accompanied us to the wedding, why a pet store would be located in such a place. Then, I began to wonder if this was a pet store for special requests. After all, it was in a beautiful, stone castle with immaculate gardens. Upon moving to China, we had had to leave our Weimaraner in the States, and I had often asked John if we might be able to get a dog in China. Sam looked at me, then John, and back to my inquisitive expression. John and Sam seemed to be understanding something that I wasn't. John said, "Come on, Ruth. Let's go on in." I remained at the windows. "But, what is this place?" Sam looked at me with the most serious expression and said, "Ruth, you are right; this is a special shop in Shanghai, but it is not a pet store. This shop is connected to the fine dining restaurant here, which is also connected with the wedding reception and catering. This is a place where many people come to get married or celebrate special occasions/ holidays. This shop is where they can select their meat and have it prepared for dinner."

The last sentence left me dumbfounded. Sam continued to talk, but I didn't hear anything else he said. I only heard his muffled explanations, as I stared into the retriever's dark brown eyes. John reached for my hand and gave a gentle tug. I followed his lead and walked, expressionless, into the reception area. I remember Daisy saying hello and me forcing a big smile, congratulating her and her new husband. I remember standing for photos and talking with some of the ladies who were in China for the first time, visiting from France. However, I don't remember much of anything else, because I just sat in a daze—a fog—questioning the facts, the differences, my reaction, and my attitude. I couldn't seem to forget what had been so bluntly explained, and I couldn't seem to understand why I so deeply rejected this concept.

Now, as I sit here and listen to John's sleep-filled breaths, I can write and reflect. In the car ride back to the hotel, I had a little bit of time to think, and now, here, I realize the crux. *Judgmental*. I am judgmental. We are all judgmental in some way. The fact that I say "we" is yet confirmation. Consider this:

A cow is an animal with four legs and bodily organs. A goat is an animal with four legs and bodily organs. A dog is an animal with four legs and bodily organs. I eat cow. I eat goat's cheese and drink the milk. I do not eat dog. I do not have a cow as a pet. I do not have a goat as a pet. I did have a dog as a pet. Where does this leave me? This leaves me sitting here in a quandary. I have an emotional attachment to a dog, and man's best friend was not deemed a cow. Therefore, because it has been proven that dogs are more 'intellectual' than cows, we are not supposed to eat them. Is this my theory? I am not suggesting that we should all go out and march along Pennsylvania Avenue to propose the sale of dog meat at our local markets; I am simply detaching myself from the emotional side of meat and aligning myself with logical deductions.

We think to eat a dog is wrong because we have them as pets. What if we all had pet chickens? What would we do then? We can't say that we don't go out and select our meat while it is still living. In America, we go fishing at stocked ponds and send it off to be prepared for dinner in a quaint country cabin. I vividly remember going to the Cross-Eyed Cricket in Tennessee, where I was thrilled to catch my first fish. The experience was promoted as an exhilarating achievement, in which I had snared my fish and would receive the rewards at the dinner table. In reality, I had caught a fish to be slaughtered and served on the table. The whole experience had been glorified and manipulated to be a moment of fun. Yes, I had fun, and I still look back on that day with fond and fun memories because I didn't see my actions—and still don't see them—as bad or disgusting or ill-intended. I was simply catching/ selecting my fish and having it sent to be prepared for dinner. Is this not the same as what I had seen tonight, here, in Shanghai? Truly, what is the difference? Again, I don't have to repeat the implications that come from this entry. In multiple journals, I have elaborated on the cultural expectations and norms for individual nationalities and ethnicities. I am tired. Maybe I should try to fall asleep counting dogs instead of sheep.

Since that day in Shanghai, I have seen every display of meat possible. I don't believe there is an animal—or part of an animal—under the sun that I haven't seen. From octopus tentacles on a stick to brains soaking in soy sauce, nothing seems to have the original shock effect that it once did. Dongbin Lu near Shenzhen Wan boasts the sight of men holding live turtles dangling from a string on the end of stick, wriggling to escape from their inverted positions. One of the most prestigious wedding ceremony hors d'oeuvres is shark-fin soup. It is as common as serving wedding cake at a traditional ceremony in the United States. Most weddings in China also wouldn't be complete without serving Peking Duck, just as most weddings in America wouldn't be complete without a special dress for the occasion. Traditional food and customary entrees are deeply embedded in social circles, as conversations and family gatherings often take place around the table. Each culture's cuisine is rooted in means of survival, availability, and tradition, which has often been practiced for more than five thousand years.

September 21, 2011—The best way to cook a turtle.

Today, someone explained the best way to cook a turtle. Who am I to question the people who have been doing it for centuries, passing the procedure from generation to generation, perfecting the savory flavor? "First," she said, "you must put the turtle in the water. Then, you turn the water on to heat. As the water gets hot, the turtle will want to drink. The turtle drinks the water, and the water gets more hot. After some time, the turtle will begin to cook itself from the inside to the outside." To me, it sounds inhumane, yet who am I to question this well-respected procedure, much like the course of action taken to prepare a turkey for Thanksgiving (excluding the moment the turkey died), as we stuff it, heat it, and eat it . . . all the while declaring, "Mmm, this is so juicy; I am so glad it's not dry this year."

Amid the questions, I found a beautiful example of one, undated, journal entry, which elaborates on the purity found within foods that are native to a region.

Dog-eating 'carnival' banned

THE government has banned a traditional carnival in Zhejiang Province in which dogs are eaten after being chopped up alive in the street following a public uproar that the festival was cruel.

The tradition in Qianxi dates back 600 years to celebrate a local military victory and is normally held every October, Xinhua said.

Vendors began to butcher dogs in public a few years ago to show their dog meat is fresh and safe, as a way to ease buyers' worry that the meat may be refrigerator-pre-served or even contaminated.

Pictures of the carnival spread via popular microblogs and had such an impact that the government gave orders that the festival be halted, Xinhua said.

"The government's response should be applauded. I hope eating dogs will become a custom there anymore," an Internet user said.

Despite once being China's bad bourgeois habit, dog meat has become increasingly popular with China's growing reputation in the past few years as food activism.

Date Unknown—The wet market.

The wet market is a place to buy a variety of fruits, vegetables, meat, and seafood. It is here that I found the best mandarin oranges I have ever tasted. The display of fruit is colorfully arranged in such a way that it beckons to be consumed. The slippery ceramic floor is wet and dirty, but above it lies an array of fruits and vegetables. It is, somehow, unique and unsullied. It reminds me of how some people can appear so beautiful, yet underneath they are filthy. Or how they can appear dirty and worn, yet be inwardly stunning. As peaches in Georgia are the sweetest by far and mangos in the Philippines are far above par, these mandarin oranges to which we all ran, were certainly unlike the ones from a can. The mandarin oranges are delicious, the stinky fruit . . . well, it's stinky . . . and the unknown fruit, which I have never seen nor know of an English name, is juicily sour. As I walk from the market with mandarins in hand, I wonder at this place . . . still often an unknown land.

April 2, 2008—Meat Hong Kong.

After lunch, we walked through an area that fascinated me, yet also made me wonder if I would be able to hold my lunch! A drizzle had begun to fall, and I watched as umbrellas began to pop a bright array of colors into the alleyways. We walked through a market with rows and rows of fruit and produce. I was struck by the vivid greens, reds, oranges, and purples which seemed to burst from each stand. As I continued to dodge the umbrellas, we came to an area where meat was for sale. Between the umbrellas, I could see unbelievable displays of fish, fresh from the ocean, still twitching! Large hunks of red meat were also displayed in open-air arenas. I could see everything from large pieces down to the smallest cuts.

We entered an area where the sale of pork dominated. I looked to my left and saw a large hook, holding the remains of a pig. The pig had been cut from head to toe, and I watched as the butcher began the cleaning process. He was pleased to see that

I was interested, and he tried to sell me the entire leg of a pig. In his stand, I saw a pig's snout, ears, feet, etc. Each piece was hanging from large chains, and none of the meat was packaged. I had been to the famous fish market in Seattle, but I hadn't been exposed to meat like this before. I kept wondering how these people prevented disease and bacteria. Eric simply said, "Do you like to cook out—y'know, barbecue?" The smells were not as bad as I suspected, but the floors of these stands were extremely slippery and the blood and fluids everywhere made me uneasy. Actually, though, I was oddly fascinated by the display and had to be urged to leave the area. I kept thinking about meat markets in the States and realizing that meat comes from animals and, although we don't usually see the behind the scenes part of meat packaging, I eat meat that was cut from an animal too, so it is not much different. As we left this area, we entered a Starbucks, and I continued to analyze my thoughts and reactions to the market. The Starbucks was a five-minute walk, yet a whole world away.

If you were handed a menu and debriefed on "specials for the evening," broiled chicken feet may not bring the same receptive reaction as broiled lobster. Why? Chicken feet don't have a reputable place in Western cultural norms. We automatically assume that eating the foot of a chicken is somehow more repulsive than eating the wing. We stand in line at the famous, local bar-b-que stand or speak about the aromatic smells of a pig that has been cured at a smokehouse, yet we are quick to stereotype and identify acceptable and unacceptable consumption of various other animal parts. What is it that causes these assumptions? The answer: cultural biases, familiarity, and norms. Being an "other" means encountering opportunities to open our eyes as well as creating an awareness of why we hold expectations and belief systems. In China, the way in which food is prepared, packaged, shipped, and consumed is quite different from customary Western experience and procedure.

the meat market

May 17, 2008 — The unexpected.

Today, after five months in China, I saw four, large black plastic bags that reminded me of the following: Despite the length of my stay, I will continue to see things that are new and different—different as it relates to the experiences I have grown to think are "common" and "normal." China will continue to reveal surprisingly unique cultural norms. I hope that I continue to experience these feelings of surprise, yet I fear it is quite possible that I may eventually become desensitized, thus missing out on erudite moments. If so, it would inhibit me from capturing the intrigue and excitement that comes with learning and sharing new things. It is precisely these experiences which easily captivate the attention of newcomers to this area of the world.

Today, we were on our way to the gym. We stepped into the elevator with five others, two of whom were lugging enormous black bags. With a total of seven people and four black garbage bags, we were unsure if we would fit on the elevator. However, in China, this is not a question. Elevators are crowded (as are most other places). The men squeezed onto the elevator with their four large bags, bumping into everyone, as if holding bowling balls while we were the unfortunate pins. I could tell by my husband's expression that he had already seen something that would send me reeling. He smirked and waited for my expected reaction. He knew that the sight would send me into a world of wonder and nausea. He had become accustomed to my all-too-common question: "Why do they do that?" Inevitably, the response: "This is China."

It was then that the smell hit me, and I looked down to see the most gut-wrenching sight. There, before me, was a dead chicken's claw, hanging limply over the edge of one of the bags. The claw's flaccid nature clearly indicated that these chickens were probably going to be served in one of the nearby restaurants. I also knew that there were only five floors in this part of the building, three of which were restaurants. The smell of dead, unpackaged chickens permeated the air, and I looked to see how many buttons on the elevator's panel had been pushed. As luck would have it, we would stop on every single floor. Each time the elevator door opened, I gasped for air, hoping that the black bags containing the lifeless claws would be hauled from the elevator. However, each time we stopped, they remained, until it was just my husband, two men, four large bags of limp chickens, claws dangling over the edge, and me.

We were going to the fifth floor, and they were going to the fourth. As the door to the fourth floor opened, the men walked directly through the restaurant with the big bags. From the way the men waddled, it was obvious that these bags were heavy. I was in awe; the men carried the chickens, along with the odor, through the restaurant and into the kitchen. In previous writings, I have observed that people in China eat the entire chicken, and I have since learned that it is an honor to eat the head, including the beak and eyes. All I can hope is that I will never be in a situation where I must defer such a privilege to the host. I cannot imagine sitting in a restaurant and watching four, big black bags of unpackaged beef pass by my table, knowing that my meal might be in one of those bags. I realize that my reactions are only a result of what I am accustomed to seeing. I realize that the bags have been a normal part of daily life in China for centuries. It is a continued cultural norm. In all actuality, it is the West that has changed, as this was also the way of original Western restaurants.

It is only my cultural expectations that lead me to feel differently about the way things are handled and/or delivered. Is it wrong of me to think that their way is outdated? Is it wrong for me to think that my ways are better? I have begun to realize that there are subconscious ways in which people may come to think that their approach is better: familiarity, comfort, expectations, etc. I wonder how often we don't take the time to look at other ways of doing things before we automatically assume that our way is best. Could these other ways be a result of cultural expectations that have been practiced over the years and become the norm—even if the norm is not necessarily the best? It may be wise to study other cultures and other ways of doing things before we jump to the conclusion that our ways are better, lest we fall into the fleeting comforts of familiarity. Would it not be better to allow some discomfort, which potentially inspires growth and change?

Our understanding of cleanliness is based on years of reports from the media, health inspections, and sanitation research; however, in recent years, much of the world has returned to the idea of organic farming. To increase their marketability and keep with the trends of the time, grocery stores have had to offer organic supplies and dedicate entire sections of the store to organic labels. In the past few decades, mass production of food has morphed from wholesome food to manufactured fodder. Farmers have begun to reintroduce the age-old idea of fresh and homegrown. Many towns are returning to the notion of hosting farmers' markets, to which numerous loyal customers flock. Although many may believe that China takes organic to a new level, we may very well learn something from some of their practices.

A few of the photos you see may stir pessimistic notions, but is this not reality? Have we forgotten that some of life is crude? Have we also forgotten that sustainability includes understanding a realist's view? Do we seek to rationalize our justifications for why these photos should be censored? This is China, life in China. The images may stir the same feelings that the photographer felt as she snapped the photo, or the writer felt as she relayed the story. Regardless, for some, reality is uncomfortable. For us, it is unaltered truth.

June 14, 2008—Chickens: frozen, thawed, whole, or partial cuts.

Here, chickens come in every shape, form, and fashion; yet I haven't had a boneless chicken breast since I arrived in China. "No bone chicken" (as my Chinese friend qualifies it) is not often offered, as it is not as healthy as the "bone chicken." Most of the time, bones are included in the meat. They are not swallowed; rather, bones are emitted from the mouth by spitting them into a small, accumulating pile next to the plate on the table. Many people in the West would find this repulsive, as the culture is not accustomed to the thought of spitting things out of the mouth during a meal. Diners do their best to ensure that there is no meat remaining on the bone when they are finished. This usually means that the sounds of sucking and slurping are commonly associated with eating chicken—chicken feet, chicken wings, chicken thighs, chicken liver, chicken head, chicken tongue—chicken everything.

chicken feet

chicken head

These things come to the forefront of my mind; today, I saw a truck loaded with chickens that had just been plucked and tossed into the back of the open-air utility vehicle. Riding in a taxi, I looked to my left and saw the large pile of pink-skinned chickens with a few feathers still randomly attached to their skins. As the taxi would pull forward, I would feel a sense of relief, knowing that I didn't have to see these poor chickens ride in the open air. However, the taxi would slow, and the truck to our left would catch up. The flopping wings of the chickens kept drawing my eyes to the merciless blue truck that hauled these birds to their destinations. I couldn't help but realize that this means of transportation would have appeared inhumane in the States, and animal rights activists as well as the Food and Drug Administration would have intercepted the truck driver with verbal accusations and possible fines. Many small farmers in the States have faced fierce sanitary sanctions for open-air poultry processing, yet these farmers are simply processing chickens in age-old ways, often in a healthier environment than that of a slaughterhouse. I'm not sure why I felt as though these chickens had been mistreated; could it be that I had been sucked into the thought that everything should be packaged in plastic and carefully transported? I quickly deducted: if people in the States saw the way that these chickens were being transported—unpackaged, in the back of an open-air truck—they may not eat chickens again. Yet, these same people, turning their noses to this picture, want organic meat and request hormone-free chickens. On first witnessing this type of poultry transportation, the reactions of foreigners would create an interesting study of perception. Where do we get our preconceived notions? Why would these chickens appear different from those plucked on an organic farm? Are we not severely shaped by media, marketing, and the masses?

We think it's normal to see a truck piled with layers of live chickens on an interstate, going to a slaughterhouse. Have you ever been behind one of these eighteen-wheelers, with feathers flying from the open-aired, wire mesh cages? How is this much different? I am not trying to stir an animal rights movement, nor do I think these juxtapositions are necessarily a reasonably concrete, tit for tat, comparison; I simply wonder, and want others to wonder, if the people in China might think our packaged chickens were strange. Would they think that the packaging and de-boning process compromises the flavor of the chicken? Would they think that freezing and shipping chickens was abnormal? I must admit: these cultural perspectives and norms as well as the reactions of others to something as simple as a chicken are quite interesting.

Knowing a foreigner's perspective is one part of the picture. However, a man living in China may wonder at the actions of foreigners as much as the foreigners question the actions of the locals. Our understanding of life is categorized and compartmentalized by the lens through which we view our world. The lens through which the Chinese view the actions of Western normalcy is also captured by their reactions, as seen in the following Chinese market man's words:

October 19, 2010 "Why is this foreigner so interested in me?"

I don't know why they find my work at this chicken stand so interesting. They stand and stare at my knife as well as the bucket into which I put the chicken. Don't they know how a chicken is prepared? Do they eat chicken? The chicken is my livelihood. They seem confused about what I am doing. Do you see these eggs? These also came from the chicken. We bring a new supply every day.

People come to this market to buy fresh meat. My chickens are from the best place in China—the countryside, away from the city. I bring them something they can't find in the supermarket. Why would anyone buy frozen things or day-old meat, when they can buy fresh meat, here? They can come in the morning, select their chicken, and I will prepare it right here, in front of them. It only takes me fifteen minutes; I am fast. The chicken is good and clean. They can take it home and eat it the same day. This is good. You don't need to worry about old meat. We are fair; we sell the meat based on the weight. Watch. I will show you. Here comes a customer.

(17 minutes later)

See how I did it. You select. We cut, prepare, and send the meat home for you to be strong. It's not hard. This is life . . . nothing too interesting. We all have to eat. Do you want one?

Everywhere in China, it is widespread and ordinary to witness these scenes, these realities. To where has normal fled? What makes us accepting or disapproving of behavior and cultures? Why are we so quick to adjudicate the opposing vantage point? In these anecdotes, there is confession, beseeching, and purity. Your next poultry purchase may bring more than a mere glance at the price; it may inspire a surplus of thoughts and reflections on cultural expectations and reactions to the norm . . . your norm.

The Population

With over 1.3 billion people, China's sheer population leaves an impression. Imagine, though, the further impact that a culture with similar physical features has on its visitors or, conversely, that visitors to China have on Chinese people. This is not to suggest that everyone in China looks the same. Chinese are just as unique to one another as Canadians. Nonetheless, straight, black hair and dark, crescent eyes are genetic features that dominate the inherited traits of Asian people. This physical norm has become a cultural norm, as it is something that identifies an entire population. The West is accustomed to genetic conglomerations, which result in a variety of hair and eye color. These observations should not be considered derogatory. Unfortunately, some may feel that these explanations are demeaning, simply because many cultures have come to label these descriptions as offensive or disparaging. Why would an explanation of simple physical features lead to a feeling of insecurity? The answer lies in the depths of what we interpret as beautiful. Our media shapes beauty and, although we hear that beauty is in the eye of the beholder, the beholder is easily influenced.

The only legitimate reason for personal discomfort may stem from insecurities. If you walked into a stadium of two million people, and you were the only person with red hair, you would probably feel one of two ways—one, awkward and uncomfortable, or two, special. In China, living as the other person in the room, both feelings tend to emerge. Again, as mentioned in the previous section, insecurity may spawn frustration and unjustifiable biases.

September 14, 2008 — Thin or fat; please don't look at that!

Previously, I have written that many of the Chinese people are interested in me and I in them, but there should be limits to our interests! As I have mentioned in my journals, the ladies' gym locker room is quite open, meaning that everyone walks around naked. I have become accustomed to this and pay no attention to those around me. The wonderful water pressure in the gym continues to draw me to daily exercise with a great shower to conclude the trip. (The shower in my apartment is horrendous — a light trickle with which I am supposed to remove the soap from my skin as well as long, naturally curly hair. If I stand upright, my head is two inches shy of the ceiling. Yes, my husband must become the hunchback of Shenzhen to bathe. Not for long, I hope.) Today, the interest in me was markedly different, and I don't imply that the actions were such that anyone was making passes or that they were trying to be offensive or rude; there is an innocent, genuine interest in me, the one who looks different. I went to the gym at an earlier time today, so there was a different group of people working out. I suspect that most of the women had the day off or were stay-at-home women.

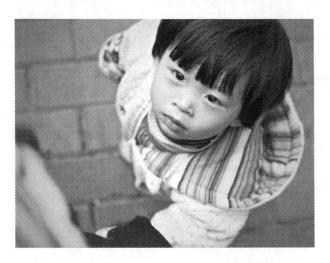

After arriving in the locker room and changing, I placed my shoes—black pumps with rather high heels—in the bottom half of the locker. One of the women in the locker room approached my locker and picked up my shoes, saying *"ahhhhh, shong tine qua ting xie fing woo ma."* This, of course, is not a literal translation, only what I heard phonetically. I had *no* idea what she was saying. She placed her hand next to the heel as if to measure it. I didn't want to take the shoe away from her, and I knew that she thought it was a very tall heel. She was simply interested in the height, but this went on for about five minutes. Five minutes is a long time to look at a shoe. (Proximity, personal space, and property is something on which I must elaborate, but I will save it for later.) Finally, I placed my hand on the shoe, and she nodded several times as I placed it back in the locker and locked the door. She watched me leave the locker room, still nodding her head. It somewhat reminded me of the awards scene in *The Sound of Music* when the second-place recipient continues to bow in appreciation.

After exercising, I quickly prepared for a shower. Before going to the showers, I stepped on the scale. Usually, people share weight with doctors, family, and, sometimes, close friends; however, today, September 14, other people were interested. When I stepped onto the scale, two women (complete strangers) scurried over to look at the reading. I quickly jumped off, thinking (and I know this is brutally honest and probably not the best choice of words): "okay, all of you genetically 'tooth-picked' ladies, whose pantlegs look like shirt sleeves . . . I cannot help it that we eat hamburgers and pizza and sweets and peanut butter and bread and drink soft drinks in colossal proportions, while you eat appropriate servings of noodles and rice and vegetables and meat and drink kegs of green tea." However, at their motioning for me to return to the scale so that they could see, I did. I suppose I felt, for a moment, like I was the entertainment, so why not? I puffed my cheeks out to imply that I was big, and the ladies laughed and shook their heads. Upon seeing 57 kilograms (126 pounds), one of the ladies provided a "thumbs up" sign. After leaving the scale and heading for the showers, I began to think about their inquisitive nature. I chuckled to myself. My first reaction was to be defensive with the attitude, "what are *you* looking at?!" Yet, as I began to wash my hair, I thought about the natural tendency to inquire about others as well as the differences we observe. I am obviously taller and built differently; I am sure that they naturally wanted to know how much a person like me weighs. I began to admit to myself that I wondered what a person who was built like them weighs. There are many features of the petite Chinese woman that I think would be wonderful to possess; however, I have been told by many of the girls who work in the office that they desire many of the features of Westerners like me.

In the midst of these thoughts, I rinsed the soap from my hair and opened my eyes. There, standing in front of my open shower stall, were four, maybe five, women. I instantly recoiled, wondering why they had come to stand in front of my stall. Yes, I was showering, but why was I on display? My first reaction was of anger and disgust. Now, I sit here and ponder the following: they were simply interested in what I looked like. Oh, the genuine intrigue of the unknown.

We don't ever really think about characteristics that we have which others may desire or want to know more about; we tend to focus on those traits that we find less appealing. Some people become so obsessed that they let it affect their happiness . . . how unfortunate. Usually, the best is pulled out of others around us, while we pull the worst out of ourselves. This should not be. The grass is not always greener. Whoever coined that phrase was intuitive. We should begin to think about the positive traits that we, as well as others, possess. This lens through which we view ourselves and others would seem to provide a much more positive view on life. Do we provide positive messages to those around us? Do our friends know that they are valued and have good characteristics? If they don't meet the standard set by someone else, do they ever get the chance to meet a standard in other areas of life? What do we base our perception of good and desirable on? What do we turn to—the job market? Television? Magazines? School? Family expectations? How can we guard against this? Can we? I would venture to say yes, we can, but it cannot be done alone, nor without diving into a metacognitive state, where we truly examine ourselves and our personal perceptions.

In the cities of China, streets never lack pedestrians, and the roads never lack vehicles. With roughly twenty percent of the world's population, China has a strong presence in the demographic arena. With massive amounts of people, it is easy for a foreigner to experience an overwhelming sense of loneliness and isolation. Standing out in a crowd may be somewhat exciting for a while, but the newness wears off quickly, and the intrigue begins to haunt each outing. Strange, isn't it? Somehow wanting to be different, yet simultaneously wanting to fit in. It can be hard to find the balance between the two and, in a community where normal no longer has a definition, identity is ambiguous, and the struggle to qualify begins.

March 19, 2010 — Yes, Dad, with you.

I just want to go outside without someone staring at me or asking to take a picture of my baby. Can I just have a normal life? Is this what celebrities feel like? If so, I don't ever want to become famous. Today, we were walking back from the overseas grocery store, and I counted at least forty-five people standing on the sidewalk ahead of me. I continued to walk through the typical crowds, hoping that we might go unnoticed. When was the last time we went unnoticed? I'm not sure I can recall a time. Each and every day that we go out, we are the object of discussion. My daughter's bright, blond curls command attention. My own father, on his first and only visit to China, was walking when a little boy came running up to him and asked, "You take picture?" My father, thinking that the young boy was asking if he would take the boy's picture, reached for the camera. Without hesitation, the young boy waved his hand, as if to say, "No, I want to take a picture with you." Dad's reaction was exactly as I expected; I had often had the same reaction at first: "Sure, I would be happy to" — while in the back of the mind, wondering "but, why?" Later, we joked about the motive of the boy's request, whether it was because of dad's great looks or his strange appearance/

presence in China. Regardless of the reason, I was glad to see that my father's jokes were actually a way of trying to grapple with something we would never know: the inner thoughts of this child as he witnessed a tall, Western man in his mid-fifties.

Unfortunately, I don't like the feelings that I am having today. I am often interested in them. Why is their interest in the West so different from my own desire to learn more about them and their ways . . . the ways of the East? Why is my way of showing interest so vastly different from their way of showing interest? Why can I simply glance, while they outright stare? Would it not be better for me to stare and get a good look, rather than having to take several, seemingly inconspicuous ganders? Are we not the same in wanting to know more about each other? Do we all desire to learn more about the unknown?

What do Chinese people think about foreign cultures? What is their perspective? If they were placed in the middle of a small Swedish village and asked to cohabitate, what would a Chinese person say or do? Ponder this idea. What would they do? How might they fit or feel alienated? Again, what is normal and commonplace for the West is quite different from normalcy in the East. The population is a vital part of the culture, a part of the norm. For the typical Chinese person in the city, seeing few people is an anomaly; for that matter, silence is new and unique. I recall an instance prior to relocating in which I caught a glimpse of one Chinese man's perspective:

December 17, 2007 — You've never heard silence?

Today, William asked me: "Ruth, where is everyone?" William is visiting from China. Upon walking out the back door and standing on the patio, William was shocked that he could stand and hear absolutely nothing. He said something that I will never forget (in his literal, yet brilliant, English translation): "I have never heard silence." His perspectives are so interesting. Having spent a few days with two of the staff from China, I am aware that the place to which I am moving is full of people. I wonder if noise and bright lights will have the same impact on me as silence and darkness has had on them.

Little did I know what I was to experience. Almost two years later, I found myself having similar questions. William's sentiments skimmed the surface of my mind and, for the first time, I felt as thought I could empathize with the other understanding. At the same time, an acute awareness emerged: if not born into a Chinese family or raised in China, the culture can never be internalized. If not born into an American family or raised in America, the culture can never be appreciated. If not born into a South African family or raised in South Africa, the culture can never be fully imbedded. Are these statements true? What do you think? If culture is the influence and culmination of experiences and our environment, how long does it take to be "fully embedded"? If we do not know it, appreciate it, recall it, internalize it, and live it, then it is foreign. When are we, then, the other person in the room?

December 23, 2009—It is eerily quiet.

Tonight, I sit in the United States, realizing that my perspective of environmental and circumstantial impact has transformed. It's dark outside, and all I can hear is a slight rustling of the trees as they gently tap the windowpane outside the window. I can hear the faint ticking of a clock from the other room and the hum of the dishwasher as it changes from one cycle to another. I don't even have a dishwasher in China. My mother-in-law's dog is curled next to my feet, and the following has poured into my mind: It took me an entire year to get used to the lights and sounds of China—the buses screeching to a halt as they carried thousands from place to place, the train below our apartment window as it chugged along the familiar route to Guangzhou, the glow of building and streetlights with Chinese characters in multiple colors. Always wondering where all these people came from, and where they could possibly be going. All of this was a part of life in the city.

from my balcony

Now, here I am, sitting in my pajamas, thinking how eerily quiet it is. I don't hear anything outside or see anyone walking down the streets in the faint glow of the one, single streetlight that I can see from this chair. Isn't it amazing how our bodies adapt to environmental and circumstantial factors? Whether we consciously realize it, we are resilient. Safe within this realization, it is easier to think of a future that holds change. What do we do to embrace change? Do we fight against the norms of one culture, thinking that we could never be like the other? Can we ever truly be like the other? Is it easier to say that we adapt to the environmental factors but not the societal ones? Is it more our environment that makes us comfortable or the people within the environment? Would we be happier living in Antarctica with our best friends or in Bora Bora, French Polynesia with complete strangers? These are all interesting things to consider; yet I wonder how many of us actually take the time to contemplate such things.

March 1, 2008 — Packed park.

I walked down two flights of stairs, passed through an underground walkway, ascended another two flights of stairs, passed the post office (which smelled of glue and freshly-shredded paper), walked past three red Chinese lanterns with unknown messages, sailed down another flight of dirty stairs, plodded through another wet walkway, and rose another flight of stairs. At the top of these stairs, I saw the park entrance, surrounded by beautiful flowers and well-kept shrubbery. This park is always bustling with activity.

Today, I have decided to sit and journal what I usually witness here. To my far right, I hear music. A small stereo plays a familiar tune, and older women have gathered to dance in unity. They must have practiced this, as their movements are fluid and unified. Separated by a small walkway on which younger children run and play, a group of musicians are playing a variety of instruments. It sounds as though they, too, have rehearsed their songs. Adjacent to the small ensemble, I see a table surrounded by six people.

They are playing some sort of game, including pieces and a board on which the pieces are played. Occasionally, loud and victorious exclamations can be heard from the game table. I can't count the number of times and places that I have seen game tables: on sidewalks, in parks, in shops, on bridges, and so on.

As I continue my scan, I see a man with a saxophone standing directly in front of me. He is only a short distance from where I sit, here on this bench, and I wonder if he is trying to draw my attention to himself. I believe the bellows from his instrument overpower everything else here. Next to the saxophonist, a small group appears to be meditating. I have no idea how they can meditate with blares from the saxophone, yet they look calm and relaxed. Next to the meditation, it looks as though a group of people, young and old, male and female, are learning a form of martial arts. They are wearing baggy clothing in matching pastel colors. To my left, I have counted eight streamers. There are eight young ladies, dressed in red clothing with bright, multicolored hats. Each is holding a streamer and performing a colorfully choreographed dance.

If I were sitting at home, reading this entry, I don't know that I would fully appreciate the diversity in my environmental sphere. Everywhere I look, people. Everywhere I go, people. Everywhere . . . people. This is China.

Like most places, China is a place of work, activity, and motion. What is at the heart of our culture? What is at the heart of communication? What is at the heart of society, tradition, and the natural environment? The answer to all of these questions is people, and this is China—a place of people.

The Family

Although interesting, compelling, and well written, I can only chuckle at a recent, somewhat controversial, Western book regarding Chinese parenting. Living here, I see the norm as the exact opposite of what this author presents, and I find the generalities to be unjustifiable. The typical Chinese mother is far from the stereotype that the Western world has so graciously bestowed. Undoubtedly, there is an elite group, which fit this author's description to a tee. I personally know seven mothers who fit the stereotypical Chinese mom. Of their children, four play the piano, two the violin, and one the cello. Their studies and extracurricular activities are carefully chosen. They follow a daily schedule, with little or no free time. I am fully aware of the expectations and guidelines these parents have, and I admire as well as respect their philosophies. Their children are extremely well versed, rehearsed, and successful, as some would classify success.

However, this is certainly not the norm in China. With a population cresting 1.3 billion, the elite groups in China who actually send their children to school are not large or influential. Although thousands may *sound* large, among a population with more than a billion, it is still quite a small percentage. Despite this, they are the ones upon whom the spotlight is focused. Regrettably, academic reporting is skewed, as it only accounts for those children who are actually attending school and, therefore, tested. Many parents, both in the rural areas of China and in many overpopulated areas of the city, do not send their children to school. On any given day, multiple children of school age can be seen playing, sleeping, and working! This is the norm. We see the accomplishments of the most elite students, yet these students are already from within an elite group. These are also the students who receive the limelight and attention, praised for their fortitude and achievements. We forget the millions who do not or cannot attend school.

April 2, 2011 — Eleven ladies sitting in a row.

I approached eleven ladies, lining the walkway of a familiar wet market. Their faces were dark and worn, showing years of wear from the weather and hard work. Their deep wrinkles were somehow beautiful, and their smiles, although missing teeth and distorted, were kind and inviting. I had wanted to talk with these women for a long time. I decided to ask them about their lives. We talked about China. We talked about their lives, why they were here, and to whom the kids that ran up and down the street belonged to. I asked if or why they did not send them to school. Here is their reply.

"Yes, every one of these kids that you see do not go to school. They cannot. They must learn our work. Some of them do not have identification because they are the second or they were born a girl. If they don't have identification, they cannot attend school, but we do not have the money to pay for identification (more than one child, you have to pay). There are at least forty kids in this block who are here every day, helping us deliver things or sending messages. This is important; school will only teach them things that limit them to one idea path, one career. But these are real experiences that will help them in everything. They will be able to do many things well."

This leads me to yet another interesting aspect of many Chinese families. Of the eight women who work in my husband's office, six have asked their mothers to move to the city to raise the child, and two have sent their children to the countryside to be raised by extended family. Shenzhen is a city with many young people. The average age in Shenzhen is less than thirty, with roughly eighty-eight percent of the population between the ages of fifteen and fifty-nine. Grandmothers come to raise the children because the mothers work. Generally speaking, the mothers are not raising their children. Just as many people in the States have more readily enrolled their children in day care programs as a result of two working parents, Chinese parents have adopted a similar standard.

It would be unwise to attack a generalization of any sort, as this entire book is a generalization, based on one environment, one perspective, in one city, in one province, within a country of more than fifty ethnic subgroups. However, these perspectives are also honest and justifiable within the current setting. Shenzhen is a fairly new city, having developed from a small, fishing village to a thriving economic hub within a mere twenty years. This, in and of itself, creates volatile and unpredictable societal dynamics. Despite these generalizations, the fact remains that many parents in Shenzhen send their children to live with relatives.

March 2, 2010 — Your child is in another province?

I took our daughter to the office today. This is the first time that she has met most of the staff. Everyone's infatuation with her curly hair made me smile, as I know that many people desire the opposite of what they are given. I wonder if my curly top will be the same. Shandra stood to the back, gazing back and forth between my daughter's little features and then mine. In her eyes, I could see something more than a fondness; it was as though she were pondering and reminiscing. It wasn't until later that she elaborated on what I had seen. During our lunch together, I recorded her thoughts:

"Sometime, I wonder why we all worked so hard. I see your small girl, and it make me miss my so much. My mom will not come to Shenzhen; she need take care of my father. I have no choices. My husband and I, we both have work. I send my son to lives there. He have more time there to do the fun things." Me: "So how long will he be there?" Shandra: "I send him for three months; maybe he come back in May. In summer, more childrens to play with, but no for sure cause no school for him to go. I do not know what I will do." Me: "I am sure you miss him more than words can describe." Shandra: "Yes. I think this life is not for long; maybe I will not continue in this way."

I felt the pain in her words, and I am reminded that generalities, accusations, and assumptions have no room here. Too many are quick to judge the actions, yet the pain remains unchanged. A mother or father who must send a child away is faced with emotional strains . . . ones that cannot be ignored or erased. How do we deal with feelings like these, when we are faced with tough decisions that seem right, yet wrong? Do we deal with them by neglecting to face reality? By justifying our responses? By displaying confidence in our choices?

With China's population at approximately 1.3 billion and the United States at 312 million, does this mean that China is four times as likely to produce a prodigy? Even with the well known one-child policy in urban areas, the population requires provisions to be made for a growing nation. The one-child policy, released in 1978, has prevented four hundred million births. Therefore, having a baby in China is no small decision, and the multiple ways in which Chinese people prepare for parenthood is calculative and full of purpose. Eight is a lucky number, so the number of births in 1998 and 2008 were higher than average. Each year is labeled according to a sign: the year of the horse, the tiger, etc. Many parents are keen on the idea of having children within the year of a desired sign, often holding multiple implications for character and success.

Despite these exciting stages of planning, hospitals and clinics have rooms which are clearly labeled, "abortion room." Abortions do not hold the same moral implications here as they do in the Western world. Abortion is not linked with any medical or religious system. To most, it is considered birth control and reactions to having met the quota. The rate is staggering. The BBC News reported that thirteen million abortions are performed each year, with some unregistered clinics that could possibly make this number higher. If so, the number of abortions per year surpasses the entire population of Belgium. The reaction to these facts is varied: some read with disgust, some with interest, and some with neutrality. Whatever the feeling, this is part of China's preparation and understanding of family and population planning. To exclude it would be to ignore one of the most prominent guidelines for Chinese families.

In the 2010 census, there was reportedly a shortage of women in China. Boys are still preferred by most Chinese parents; therefore, it is against the law to learn of your unborn child's gender. With some coaxing as well as monetary rewards, however, it is possible to obtain this information. If able to afford it, parents may purchase the right to have a second child in an urban area. Children who are born without certification, however, are often unable to attend school or be a registered entity in China. If a person is told they can have as many children as they would like, will they not consider their options, and some decide to have none, some two, five, or seven? On the other hand, if a person is told they can only have one, is it not likely that they will have that one? If twenty million women have only one, though, this is still an additional twenty million people. The numbers are overwhelming. It is also logical to consider the assumed stereotypical struggles and benefits of being an only child—not a topic on which I will elaborate in this book. Although a typical "only child syndrome" stereotype is that they are spoiled, when it comes to labor and delivery, spoiled would not be the correct choice of words.

May 2011—Wait until the last moment. Otherwise . . .

Today, a dear friend of mine was describing her recent birthing experience in Shenzhen. Although I gave birth to my first child in Hong Kong, it pales in comparison with her elaborate description of the experiences on the mainland. Much like the concept of wards in older, American hospitals, Chinese women labor in a common hall. Once you have reached the point of delivery, you are taken to a private room. Today, with wide eyes, she explained, "My water broke while I was in the bed, and I labored as long as I possibly could at home, because my sister has had two children in China, and she told me what to expect. I labored until my contractions were extremely close; then I went to the hospital and delivered within two hours. I didn't have to labor in the common area, as I was already dilated seven centimeters, but I saw it. Many women, side by side, were laboring together. Each one would go through a contraction, but somehow, I don't think it was as shocking as I expected it to be. Women who are laboring don't think about their environment very much. They simply think about the task at hand."

She continued by explaining that the staff wanted to know if she had the "proper documentation" from the government, allowing her to have a second child. I wonder what they would have done if she had said no. Would they have asked her to leave while laboring? I was glad to hear that a colleague of the nurse who had asked said, "She doesn't need this form; can't you see that the rules don't apply to her? She is not Chinese."

Another friend's experience with placentas in a Shenzhen hospital led her to conclude that typical precautions for the disposal of biohazard material are not always paramount. She watched as a dripping bag of them was hauled to the hallway and placed in an oversized trash bin.

Like everything else here, there are fundamental things that remain the same. All women give birth in basically the same way. However, the environment varies tremendously. If a snapshot of delivery rooms or wards from across the world were taken today, in 2011, what would we see? Someone should do this and develop the results.

Regardless of the environment, births are abundant in China. For many in Shenzhen, birth is the beginning of family dependency and interaction. Grandmothers move to the cities, and *ayis* (the Chinese word for aunt, yet in this case often unrelated and employed as a nanny) are hired to take care of young children. Often, grandmothers and Ayis take care of the children, clean the house, cook the meals, wash the dishes, do the shopping, and tend the laundering needs. Abundant both among the local people and the expatriate community, the ayis are a vital part of the modern Shenzhen family.

October 11, 2011— "And she told me . . . ayi."

(This entry is told by a fellow expatriate in its pure form, unedited and written with English as a second language.)

Ayi, nanny, maid, helper . . . whatever you call her, in almost every country, it means the same. I don't know where to start to describe my opinion about Chinese ayis (aunt/nanny). Usually, people (not only in my country) see mothers who have a nanny (let's use that term for the time being) as either bad mothers, meaning less capable, not caring mothers, too career oriented, etc. or have to face jealousy from other mothers who cannot afford this comfort. With every stereotype, there is usually partial truth. It must be coming from somewhere. Stereotypes are good. If not, there would be too many things to think every day. We would not manage. Luckily life is not only black and white. It is like a good black and white picture, to have it nice, lots of shades of gray have to be there, too. I am not so smart; someone smarter said it before me, but I completely agree. There are mothers who can manage themselves, either they want to and they can or they have to. No other option is there for them. Some are lucky to have helpful parents living close to them who are not working full time anymore and are still healthy. Living in China, thousand kilometers far from my family, this is not my case.

I am a mother of three kids. After the second one, I always had a nanny to help me. She helped me to be able go to work (I did not have to), to help me to rest, to clean, to cook (I love to cook but not every day), to do grocery shopping, to help me to study with the older ones, to [allow me to] breastfeed the younger one while she was studying with the older one, to help me to have moments for myself, to allow me and my husband to go out for dinner or to sleep longer on Saturday and many more things, but mainly to be a better mother. But that was in my country, she spoke the same language. I knew her for a long time. Our families knew each other for a long time. It was nice. Really. I know, I have to admit my case is not within the majority. I did not forget.

Coming pregnant to China, I did not have a job, of course, and I did not plan to search for a job for a long time. So, my plan was to manage myself. Suddenly I had lot of time. One day, I got sick. My husband was away for a few days. Work. I was alone with two kids and big belly attached to bed not being able to even eat. Do not forget that I did not speak a word of Chinese and no family or friends were close to help me. We were newcomers. I remembered the offer from one Polish family: "Do you want the sister of our ayi to work for you? Maybe you should find one. Everyone has an ayi. They are good and cheap." I did not want. I did not know her! I did not understand her. They for sure have strange habits (which I already had a chance to notice in the streets). However, now I wanted her to be there. To cook for kids, to bring me tea, to call doctor. We managed: my son, the oldest, was bringing me food and making cereals for his younger sister for a few days. Good boy. One week later, he got sick from me. I felt guilty. *C'est la vie.* Only cold . . . however, it was not necessary. This time ayi was taking care of him to protect me not to catch it back. You are pregnant, she said. I did not understand her talk, but her finger pointing at my huge belly was more than clear to me.

She has been with us more than two years now. During this period she made our stay in China much easier. Not only by taking care of kids and cleaning house and cooking and shopping and teaching kids to speak Chinese. My Chinese is poor, but ayi became our eyes, she is our speaker. She sees what is happening at home and she can deal with the other world and solve things in our favor, our interest. For example, new microwave is broken. She calls the number and can claim the product. No need for us to go there and face another frustrating situation trying to claim the product. Might be a stupid thing. Yes, I agree. There is lot of small, so called stupid things in life, but even what we may think is stupid may still help us learn something.

this is my ayi

4/11/08 — Revealing what?

Today is my brother's birthday. I wish that I could speak with him to tell him happy birthday and I love you, but when I called, the mobile phone sent me to voice mail. It is funny how a simple recording of someone's voice can cause such feelings of homesickness. I hope that he has had a great day. When I told a few of the girls in the office that today was his birthday, they were eager to know if he was going to receive presents and a party. I asked them if families in China celebrate birthdays with presents and parties, to which they replied, "It seems that Americans celebrate more with presents more than with family." I thought this was interesting. I learned that Chinese birthdays, for those who are older, are usually approximations, while the younger generations have exact records and documentation of birthdates. I also learned that many gather, but gift giving is not a standard practice. It has only been within recent years, as China learns more about Western customs, that giving gifts has been a part of birthday celebrations. I told them that my brother would probably receive gifts from family and may have a nice dinner, but I had grown up understanding that parties were typically for young children as well as given for decade birthdays, such as when people turn thirty, forty, or fifty. To this, they mentioned the significance of the red envelope, in which money is enclosed for special occasions. This discussion continued into the idea of parties and celebrations.

I began to think about their understanding that we celebrate more with presents than with family. I was saddened by the message that may be coming from American/Western culture. Do we send the message that things are more important than people? Is our image marred by materialistic obsessions? I wonder if most of the world views Americans as selfish or selfless, family-oriented or material-oriented? What are we? How are we defined? How do we define others? How can we ensure that these definitions are true depictions of who and what we are and stand for?

Tonight, I went to dinner with two of the girls from the office. At dinner, the girls began to inquire about America as well as offer their understanding of American culture. At times, I was shocked by the generalizations, yet reminded that I, too, had made generalizations about Chinese culture based on things I had seen and heard here. Therefore, my feelings of shock turned to feelings of understanding. Mindy explained that she thought American women were more open than Chinese women. I asked what she meant by "more open." Mindy explained that American women seem to wear more revealing clothing by letting their chests show as well as their stomachs. I asked her if there were women in China who showed these areas of their bodies, to which she explained, "there are some women, but it is not viewed as acceptable." We went on to talk about more "openness" observations.

Hilary asked why women in music videos wear lingerie and kiss on many men. This question sent me through a whirlwind of thoughts! I asked her if these videos and other media like it were where they received most of their understanding of American culture, to which they both responded, yes. I explained that television is not always an accurate depiction of an entire nation or the way in which families function. Hilary still replied, and I will never forget it, "I think you and John must be more Chinese than American. I don't think you are like most Americans." I have no idea why she made this statement. Was it because I was wearing a three quarter length turtleneck with a covered midsection? I didn't know whether to feel offended or complimented. After their perceptions, I wanted to feel complimented, but my roots forced me to feel defensive and somewhat protective of my homeland. Even as I write now, I feel myself struggling with my reaction to this statement. I wish that we could all fit into a category besides nationalities. I hope that we think about the messages we are sending to those around us: in work, in schools, in life, etc. I hope that the way we are viewed is a true summary of how we think that we should be living as well as how we perceive ourselves.

The Transportation

How do you get to work? Do you drive? Do you take a bus? Do you take a taxi or use the subway system? Are you close enough to walk? Have you ever ridden a bicycle to work? Have you ever walked home with your groceries? Do you buy only what you can carry home from the grocery store, or do you buy as much as possible, cutting down on the number of trips to the store, and stack everything you purchase in the back of the car?

Transportation: it impacts many aspects of daily life. It influences and changes the way we spend our time. In China, transportation plays a major role in the expenditure of time as well as managing daily priorities. Before 1997, more bicycles had been made for the Chinese market than all other countries combined. With a massive and growing population, there came a need for multiple ways by which to move large amounts of people, quickly and effectively. China has much to teach the West about transporting crowds.

October 12, 2008 — Never look before you cross.

Today, I walked to a nearby park. To get there, I must walk three blocks. Within these three blocks, I come to a crosswalk, a pedestrian overpass, a subway entrance and exit (which leads me under the intersection through a tunnel-like, pedestrian walkway), and a set of outdoor escalators. I wonder how many escalators are in this city; the number must be somewhere in the hundreds, maybe thousands. Do escalators rust in the rain? (I digress.)

I found myself in awe of the way in which provisions have been made for cyclists. Each set of stairs (and they are everywhere) also has a concrete ramp which bicycles and carts can easily traverse. I have been told that at one time, there were over seven hundred million bicycles in China. Can you imagine? I can see where these numbers have influenced the architectural engineering and design of places that require walkways. Today, not only did I see bicycles ascending and descending these slopes, but also a multitude of supplies for various destinations. I witnessed someone moving a big-screen television. This television was strapped to the back of a bicycle, precariously balanced and completely foreign to any of my experiences of moving a television. Can you picture it? It's not easy for someone to imagine such a scene or even to believe it. Where was he going with it?

briefing

advertising

Styrofoam

I saw at least eleven three-wheeled carts, some hand-pulled and some motorized. I wanted to know about each one. I saw enormous piles of packaging supplies. What were they going to do with such large piles of Styrofoam? What was in the red buckets, dangling from either end of a pole, which was balanced across a man's shoulders? Some people, in typical storybook-fashion, were carrying fruit in large baskets—fruit which I never knew existed until I moved to China: the dragon fruit. Today, I am reminded that most of the people in China are adroit and skillful at packaging and moving things from one place to another. Their ability to transport goods and make handles for boxes with mere twine or tape has instilled an odd, unexplained admiration. Why do we admire people? What inspires admiration? Is it what we value and consider to be talent? Is this something that is too subjective? Is the word *admiration* an appropriate word for this context? I'm not sure how to classify my views on the Chinese style of moving or relocating things. Awe? Wonderment? Appreciation? It is hard to confine and label the feelings.

All around me, I see movement. The buses are loud; the bicycles are dangerous. It appears as though there is little regard for proximity. Could this be because of the hordes of people? Could it be that they bump into me and never look before they cross because they don't have to wonder if someone is there. Odds are, there is someone there; there is always someone there. This is China. No matter where you go, there are people, and these people are trying to get to somewhere else. Therefore, why is it necessary to look? If they look, they are wasting time. Step out; don't worry about defensive driving or mannerisms . . . . This is a complete shift from the lessons of the West. Some have speculated that it is the "only child syndrome," which suggests that because most of the people in China come from a family in which they are the only child, they subconsciously think they are the most important. Having always received what they wanted in the home, why should they not be first along the streets in the city as well? (Again, a digression, but one at which one might stop to ponder.) A more accurate description from the Chinese people may be, "It is against the law to hit a pedestrian; if you look before you cross, then you are responsible if the car hits you; but if you don't look, they are responsible for hitting you. It would be their fault if you didn't look at them, because you didn't see them." All I can muster is . . . *wow!*

Regardless, there is something interesting about the way in which transportation may identify a particular culture. Would you transport your mattress, precariously balanced, on your moped? Would you pull an armoire on a small wooden dolly attached to your bicycle, all the while maneuvering between cars, vans, and buses? Would you use a bicycle to move your television from one residence to the next? Do you even own a bicycle? Do these examples sound ridiculous and fabricated? They are not. In China, this is ordinary.

May 1, 2011 — It is amazing how much I have become desensitized to these scenes, as they no longer seem so absurd. As of late, I am rarely drawn to these oddities. And a seatbelt? What is a seatbelt? Although young children sit on laps in the front seat without a seatbelt, I somehow shake my head in disapproval and accept it as TIC; whereas, I would gasp and call the authorities back home.

In China, just as in the West, many people spend one fifth of their working day simply trying to get to and from work. However, there is a difference in China. One is more likely to experience the following hypothetical situation: You've left your office and arrived at the familiar bus stop. As you see your bus approaching, you release a sigh of exasperation. You already know the scene that will follow. The doors will open, people will fall out of the bus, not due to their exiting the bus, but because they must alight from the pushing forces from within. You watch as the passengers immediately step back on to the bus, hoping that the doors will magically enclose them into the small space they require. With less than three inches between the passengers' faces, you watch as your mode of transportation passes you by, and you wait another fifteen minutes for the next bus.

You know that rush hour may require patience, as transportation times are often tripled. You also know that the time spent on the bus would be a great time to check e-mail and get ahead, yet the luxury of having a seat doesn't even allow space for a laptop or handheld device. Based on experience, nothing can be accomplished on the bus; with a slight turn or sudden stop, people will fall on you. Others have often squeezed between your seat and the seat in front of you, just to make room for additional passengers. No, the time to and from each spot seems wasted and useless. To someone in the West, it may become frustrating. To the person from China, it is part of the environment, the culture, and . . . it has become the way of life. Venture to believe that cultural awareness and acceptance might make life more meaningful and enjoyable to the ones who seek to understand and respect a place where space is a luxury.

December 28, 2007—Am I invisible?

I am jotting this down as I stand in a clump of people. This is the only way I can think to describe them, as I have been standing here for quite some time, trying to decide where the semblance of a line begins or ends. I simply want to get into a taxi. I thought I was standing in the taxi line, but every time I think the next one is for me, someone rushes in to jump in the backseat. Is this place void of proper queues? They have pushed me out of the way; rushed on to elevators before I had a chance to alight; crammed against me on the metro line; and now jumped ahead of me to get the next taxi. Am I supposed to be rude? Should I push next time? Is it the only way to survive here? How can I drop every social rule I have learned? This is not easy, but I've got to put this pen and pad down now and push, or I will never get a cab.

When it comes to transportation, China's sheer numbers leave no room for hesitation or hospitality. Those who hesitate will stand for hours waiting for a queue. Hospitality is reserved for the home and business ventures. Transportation, however, is in a league of its own. Rather than in frustration or abrasive behaviors, drivers often use their horns to let you know they are there, as they are all trying to get ahead or arrive first. Without this mentality, one would wait forever.

February 21, 2009 — Pulling a mule across Binhai Road.

It has taken me one hour and twenty-five minutes to get from one side of the city to the other on this bus, and I am still about ten minutes from my destination. The K204 bus is a great way to travel between LuoHu and Shekou, but this is a bit too much. Back home, I would have been in an entirely different state by now; here, I am still in the same Chinese city, and we have been driving steadily for a while. I miss being able to hop in the car and drive to the store.

Wait; we've stopped. Do you know why? There is a donkey in the middle of the road. In a city of fourteen million people, with busy streets and bustling crowds, a man has decided to bring his wares to the streets. I would venture to say that this city is a gathering place for the old and new generations. To my right, I see a BMW, snuggled between a big, blue delivery truck and a taxi. What do I hear? Our bus driver is yelling at the man who is pulling the donkey across the busy Binhai highway at a snail's pace. However, in an intriguing sort of way, the Chinese man is sweet and calm. He doesn't reciprocate the tonal exclamations that come from the driver, nor does he provide crude gestures toward the horns that so loudly echo in chorus, beckoning him to get out of the way. Contrarily, as he slowly makes his way across the remainder of his course, he lifts his head and politely nods. This man is simply transporting his goods, just as the bus driver is transporting his. Wow! A moment for me to sit and reflect. . . . Here, on this bus, I am the only one like myself. Out there, on the road, he is the only one like himself. As the horns continue to blare and the donkey plods along, I can only smile, knowing that in some strange way, I am much like the man with the donkey . . . out of place in China.

Why are we so quick to judge transportation as well as the speed with which it is accomplished? If the job is done well, does it matter by which means it is completed? We hear news of a more aerodynamic car or a faster airplane. We speak of the value found in advances and technological discoveries, yet we often forget to recognize the value of each and every person with whom we come in contact. No matter how miniscule we perceive the aspiration to be, do we value people? Have improving modes of transportation been advertently linked to success? I'm not necessarily attacking our nature, but I believe we often place levels on success, somehow often thinking that one person's goals and objectives should be esteemed beyond another's. Is this good? Should we, even though we know it is based on what we value and the perceptions we have, do this? Is it possible to completely disregard our innate nature and biases toward what we believe are examples of success? . . . And all of these thought-provoking questions by witnessing a few modes of transportation and the length of time it takes to accomplish a goal.

May 4, 2008—My fingers are red and blue.

I bought too many groceries today, and I could barely make it back to the apartment. I don't have a car, so I must consider weight limits. After meandering through the aisles and searching for anything familiar on the shelves, I found a few things that I recognized. However, after an hour in the store, I exited the mall with five plastic shopping bags. As I walked up the ramp toward the street level, I glanced down to see the tips of my fingers becoming deep, deep red. My purse was barely dangling from the edge of my shoulder bone, and I knew that, at any minute, it would careen down my arm and put additional strain on my wrist. Where was my car?

To make things worse, summer had already decided to show its face. I was wearing blue jeans and a light blue, short-sleeved shirt. By the time I reached the next block, the light blue shirt had transformed into a light blue shirt with navy blotches; the sweat was beginning to pour down my cheeks and drip onto my shirt. Of course, the areas in which sweat likes to pool creates this deeply attractive state. Finally back in my building, I dropped the bags in the elevator, only to see deep, white blisters like snow-capped mountains, which had formed amid red and blue fingers and palms. What had I done to myself? I would never attempt this again. Would someone from China, accustomed to transporting her groceries and supplies on foot, ever have attempted this? Do the Chinese buy groceries every day? Do they buy things each day because they want everything to be fresh, or because they can't carry everything? Oh, if only I could speak fluently, I would ask a trillion questions.

One Year Later: I have since learned that I do not have to carry my groceries, as I can enlist delivery services. Delivery has become such a vital part of life in China that an entire chapter, as you will see, has been dedicated to this concept.)

evening snack

In China, within a space of twenty square feet, it is not uncommon to see five or six modes of transportation: a car, a cart, a taxi, a bicycle, a scooter, a bus, and the entrance to a subway station. Slowly, transportation becomes embedded in culture. In America, owning a car is more about being able to get from one place to another. In China, owning a car is still recognized primarily as a status symbol. This city is a mixture of old and new. It is not unusual for a visitor to China to observe fruit being carried in baskets, the bearer weaving between the latest Mercedes Benz at a stoplight.

The number of people in China who own a car is increasing exponentially. If the trend continues, there will be too many cars and not enough space for all of them. A Chinese man in an international office told me that it's highly likely that the trend will continue:

September 19, 2010 — Owning a car is entitling.

"Ruth, it's not that I don't think having a car would be the greatest thing for my family's reputation, but I am afraid that I could not afford the car or take the time to prepare for the driver's test. There are over one hundred pages in the study guide. You see, if I want to buy a car, I would be adding to the cars on the road. Traffic is already bad here. I think the subway is okay, and they are opening new stations each month. But I know that owning a car is the next step."

Although I haven't had time to adequately understand his explanation, I see that he feels as though owning a car is entitling. Again, this demonstrates the differences in cultural norms. Unless a person in the West is buying a luxury sports car to demonstrate wealth, the majority of vehicles are purchased because there is a need to transport people or things. In addition, with the exception of cities, public transportation in the West is not abundant; therefore, necessity becomes the motive for purchasing. At what point do needs as well as wants become part of a cultural expectation? Americans expect to have a car because there are few ways to get from place to place. The Chinese are provided with multiple transportation options, yet the people want to own a car. At what point do societal needs and expectations become an integral part of the culture? Or do they?

When was the last time you rode a bicycle to work? When was the last time you witnessed a man pulling a donkey across the street in front of your bus? These things make us think about the personal expectations of our transportation culture. We may be quick to make assumptions about acceptable and unacceptable methods of transportation. Who or what defines what is acceptable?

The Work

Within a short twenty years, Shenzhen's population soared from less than one million to over ten million. After Shenzhen was deemed a special economic zone, the number of migrant workers and business gurus infiltrating the area grew exponentially. It was, and still is in many ways, a hub for innovation and new business. Just over seventy percent of the city's population is from a variety of other provinces; therefore, it has also been difficult to place an exact and accurate number on the actual number of people within the expanding city limits. Due to rapid growth and the original infrastructure, many events in Shenzhen have provided models and lessons for other growing metropolitan areas. Shenzhen continues to grow and develop, and the construction of various structures remains a prominent sight on the city's skyline. As someone arrives from Hong Kong, across the Shenzhen Bay Bridge (Shenzhen Wan), Di Wang (formerly the tallest building in Shenzhen) is now being surpassed by yet another enormous structure called Jin Ji Yi Bai.

With all of the growth, one might be able to believe that construction sites are erupting everywhere. In every district, on almost every corner, scaffolding covered in green canvas engulfs large concrete and steel structures. Large Caterpillars and cranes with jackhammers and cement trucks roll from site to site, thrusting concrete toward the sky at rapid rates. It took less than one year to complete an apartment complex which contained sixty floors of apartment space; some floors containing more than four apartment units. It is mind-boggling to know that the population of the apartment complex where I live is the equivalent of the entire town in the United States from which I moved. The population of the greater Shenzhen area is equivalent to the state of Georgia's entire population.

The work that has evolved from such growth is a compilation of old and new experiences. Skilled labor is just as important as professional expertise. Not often is there a balance between the two; however, here, there are unique expectations and requirements for the increase in numbers. Sometimes, the way in which they work is uncultivated and uncalculated.

September 4, 2011—Sure, just dangle from the thirty-first floor.

Beginning at dusk, with an air conditioning unit attached to his belt, his belt attached to a rope, his rope attached to a carabineer, and his carabineer attached to a hinge on the window, he began to replace our unit. After three visits to our home, this repairman finally realized that the air coming from the vent is not cold. Despite the fact that we had explained it multiple times, in multiple ways, he truly believed that, each time, he had fixed the problem. Finally, two days ago, he said, "Yes, I think we need to change it. You need a new one." Mustering a polite grin, I simply replied, "Yes, you are right. We do."

bamboo sticks

Now, I am sitting in the hallway, writing this and watching the man as he has climbed out the window to the floor above us and hangs from the thirty-first floor of the apartment complex. There is nothing below him, and the sun is going down. I am sitting here so that I can keep my child from watching what he is doing. Each time she comes near her room, which is where he is working, I distract her with something in the living area. I would dread the idea of her attempting to mimic his actions, which seem absurd and completely unorthodox.

He probably weighs less than a hundred pounds, and he is holding an air conditioner which has been passed to him by an assistant. There is no easy way to get to the place where he must exchange the broken unit for the new one. I can't watch.

It has been ten minutes, and now the man is holding his cell phone with one hand. He isn't speaking into the receiver. No, he is using the glow of the cell phone to act as a light. The sun has descended, and it is dark. With one hand he holds his phone, and with the other he precariously tries to attach important electrical wires. I have never seen anything like this in my life. I hope he survives this on-duty call. I can't decide if I admire him for his bravery (which I could never exhibit) or if I think he is utterly dim-witted to attempt such a feat.

At times, I have felt like the man who is holding the air conditioner, and at other times, I have felt like the air conditioner, dangling by a thread. I can't elaborate now, but suffice it to say that there are times that we all feel as though we are dangling something or we are the one being dangled. Today will be a day that I never forget, and I will never again look at an air-conditioning unit the same way.

Shenzhen, like many cities in China, has had to consider the job market. With such an enormous population, the number of jobs must increase, and multitudes of people need something to do, so Shenzhen has risen to the occasion. There are jobs for practically any type of service. At the bank, someone has been hired to push the "take a number" button. If you try to push it yourself, you have taken away the job of someone who is paid to do it, thus possibly insulting that employee. Multiple people are hired to sweep the water. When it rains, street sweepers emerge to ensure that rainwater is swept to the nearest drainage system. It is quite clear that these workers take their jobs seriously. At most salons, one person takes your bag and provides you with a robe; one person asks you if you would like coffee or tea; one person applies hair color (if you color your hair); one person washes your hair, and another styles it. Therefore, it is possible that you have just helped five people hold a job in China. Maybe the most interesting job seen to date is buffing the concrete/marble mixture.

May 1, 2008—Like in the school hallway, but buffing the sidewalks?

I had to take a picture, because I know that no one will ever believe me. I will try to explain, but they will think I am exaggerating. Today, as I was walking back to the gym, I could see small cones, placed as barriers, along the marble and stone walkways. From a distance, I saw the most confusing events taking place. The machine that is used at the beginning of each school year (with an enormous rotating buffer pad and one handle that jars the entire body when held) to buff and polish the floors stood in the midst of bubbles. I approached and wrote the following on the back of an envelope in my bag: "They are buffing the marble walkways, and these walkways are outside. I am watching three men, each with his individual responsibility. One man pours sudsy water from a large red bucket on to the walkway. The second man pushes the rotating electrical buffer along the outdoor walkway, and the third man follows the machine, spraying the residue with a water hose and nozzle. It hasn't been five months since I saw these machines being used at the middle school before welcoming students back from the holidays. However, these machines were indoors, and I cannot imagine the reactions if the janitors had hauled the machines to the front of the building to buff the sidewalks. I am baffled. Why are they doing this?"

I suppose I may never know why they were doing this, but I can imagine the men were hired to do the job, and they felt satisfied with their contribution to the maintenance of the facilities. Whatever the reason, they have a job, and I can see that they take it seriously. Do we take our jobs seriously? Even the ones that are considered to be small tasks? Would we put forth the same amount of effort for each responsibility, or do we esteem some jobs above others?

China has interesting pep talks for employees, which commence at the beginning of each shift. This important meeting includes well-formed lines in front of which the manager for that particular shift stands and calls the roll. He/she also provides important instructions and reminders. In quite militaristic fashion, employees conclude the meeting with a chant or unified reply.

June 4, 2008—Every day at 5:00 . . . saaaalute!

I look forward to this time of day, as I know that my husband will soon be home and seclusion will end. I haven't easily adapted to Luohu, but I know that life here will get better. Adaptation is a peculiar process.

The days are getting warmer, and I have found a great group of expatriates in Shekou. I wish it didn't take more than forty-five minutes to get there and back, yet I shouldn't complain. There are many things for which I should be grateful: running water (yes, I have to hunch over in my shower and hold my own shower head), food (yes, I have to buy a gallon of milk that costs $12.00, hoping that it was actually imported rather than simply bearing a good copy of the label), clothing (yes, although at a size 6, I am comfortably a medium in America, yet I am an XXL in the Chinese stores), and shelter (yes, I have water leaking from the ceiling and molding clothing because of moisture). I write this a bit too casually, as I am fully aware that multitudes of people live without the comforts of clean water, shelter, shoes, or any food at all. Gratefulness is something we all, at times, lack.

I sit in the window seat of our studio apartment, staring out over the skyline. To my right is the large Bank of China building with the familiar train tracks that separate me from Dongmen, and I can see the horseshoe-shaped overpass that takes me to my husband's office off of Shennan Road. I have come to welcome a familiar site below. On the street, from our twenty-second floor home, a daily activity draws me to perch myself in this familiar spot and gander. I have taken pictures and given adequate space in my journals to the timely appearance of the workers at this particular "hot pot" restaurant, below. I have even gone so far as to buy water at a nearby convenience store, so that I could purposely walk past their carefully, formed lines.

Today, I have taken my spot on the window seat; it is precisely 4:58, and I know that just two minutes separate me from the intrigue of their habitually unusual, yet somehow mesmerizing activity. I already know that twenty-four people will emerge, marching along in a straight line as stiff as soldiers, to form four rows of six: four of these people will look like hostesses in crimson dresses, and these ladies along with two women in gold dresses will stand on the front row; the second row will be filled with men in black pants and white shirts; six men with tall, white chef's hats will stand at the back. Standing in front of these people will be two people wearing suits. Each of them will be holding a clipboard and speaking very quickly in Mandarin. Then, although it looks as though they have evacuated the building, they will remain calm while instructions are given and exercises begin.

At the conclusion of whatever it is they are doing, the group will march back into the restaurant. After that, I only know that I won't see them again until tomorrow at 5:00 p.m. Since my time observing this daily occurrence, I have seen instructions to security staff and other employees in spas, salons, and other eateries. It is as if they are receiving instructions and a pep talk.

Here they come. I watch. As expected, they are here again. I wonder if they receive new instructions or if this is monotonous to those who work there. I wonder what is said. I wonder if most shops in China do this. Do other stores commence their meetings behind doors? It may be a good idea to adopt this type of daily gathering. They begin the exercise portion of the meeting with arm circles. Following the circles, the members begin to conduct stretching exercises. After stretching comes the jumping jacks, leg stretches, neck rolls, jogging in place, and returning to large arm circles. They are simply stretching before work. I wonder how many companies would benefit from a pep talk and stretch session. Company yoga, anyone? Some people walk into their offices and never see, hear, or converse with others. I think it would be good to talk with someone in China about this meeting. It would be good to know more.

Yes, Chinese people take their work seriously, and this may be the reason they have managed to perfect each individual craft. Generally speaking, they are hard working and committed to their jobs. Like anywhere, they like to feel needed and appreciated. With such a large population, scavengers and recyclers find that their services are certainly needed and appreciated. Every evening at 12:30 a.m., a large truck comes to the fishing port and picks up enormous bundles of Styrofoam. Every night, it is also common to see pile upon pile of cardboard being gathered and carted from place to place. From where the Styrofoam and cardboard comes as well as to where it is going, most do not know. It appears that there is always a flurry of activity.

September 22, 2011—Scavengers galore.

For years I have noticed it, but I don't think I have ever written about it. Everywhere I go, I see people salvaging materials. At least three times a week, on the corner of Wanghai and JinShiJi, someone is dissecting an old television or removing buttons from old keyboards. I've seen piles of old batteries, shoes, wrenches, rusted bolts, remote controls, and other unidentifiable remnants.

Something else I have noticed: every day, the same lady sits near the entrance of the convenience store at the base of Nan Hai Mei Gui Yuan. Each day, she pedals her three-wheeled cart to the apartment complex and waits for recyclables. I have seen her coming with an empty cart and leaving with a wide variety of plastic bottles, cans, boxes, containers, etc., often piled high above her head. I wonder if she knows that the cereal box in her stack may have come from my apartment. I wonder if she has ever tasted Cheerios. I wonder where she takes everything. I wonder what it will be used for. I know she is compensated for her collection, but I wonder how much she receives for a stack such as this.

Everywhere I look, when I actually stop and pay attention, there are scavengers. Some are reusing discarded cooking oil; some are taking electronics apart; some are collecting recyclables. I have been told that there is a well-established system in place for scavenging. Whatever they are doing and whatever system has been put in place, it seems to work. It would be interesting to have a discussion with one of these people who collect, dissect, transport, and deliver . . . if only I could speak the language. Is anyone else interested in knowing more about them? Am I somehow odd for wanting to know? Should I simply live and let be? I might learn from them. They might learn from me. Regardless, here I sit, watching another stack of plywood pass by.

April 8, 2008—A beautiful wrinkle.

As I walked to the office, I saw an elderly man pulling a cart. The cart reminded me of the one in *Fiddler on the Roof.* Its wheels were moving, yet they barely made a full rotation within the span of thirty seconds. The man wore baggy burlap pants, paired with a worn blue shirt. He had a skinny gray beard and the weathered, wrinkled face of a Chinese man. I slowed when I saw him, thinking to myself, "even in the midst of his humble demeanor and feeble nature, he is a beautiful sight." I was touched by the picture before me. He is what I would imagine to be a glimpse into the past and origins of this small, fishing-village-turned-megametropolis. I wondered how much he has seen in life . . . about his stories. I wished that I could sit and talk with him for hours. He was unaware of me or my ganders as he methodically, with down-turned head, focused on each step forward. I also wondered at the age of this man. As we finally passed, I could see that he was pulling pieces of scrap wood. I had seen these carts, lined along new shops. While the new shops were being designed, men would come and ask for the scraps from any constructed displays. Stores come and go here, and each month a business is closing or opening. The interiors are often changing, and eager men and women are there to retrieve discarded materials. I wonder how they use the scraps. My thoughts returned to the old man as I passed a new shop, wondering if he was fortifying a home, carving a nice piece of furniture, storing it for winter, or what.

scavengers

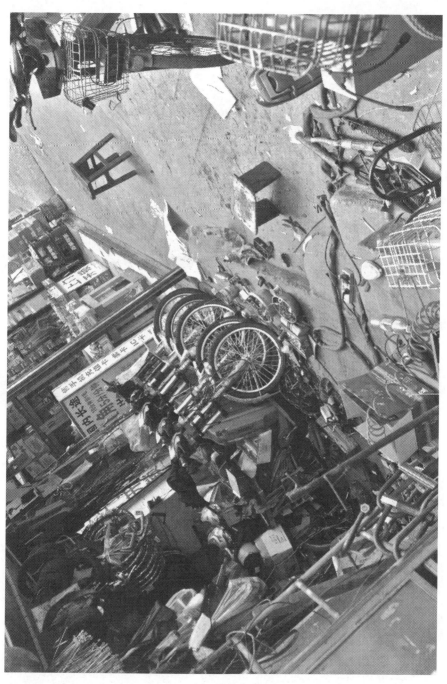

mechanic shop

November 7, 2008 — Everywhere we look: work, work, work.

On every side, I see construction, and now they are filling in the sea. Like little worker bees, it appears they never rest. This city is catapulting into high rises. I don't know how the population could possibly continue to increase; but they continue to build, so I suppose the people will continue to come. My husband seems to think the reason that the sea level is rising is not due to global warming, but the formation of reclaimed land. It could be true. The place to which we are moving used to be in the ocean. Along the southern seaboard, apartment complexes and office space is exploding. As holes and basements are unearthed for skyscrapers, the soil is delivered to the coastline, where more land may be formed and expansion of the border continues. I wonder if Shenzhen will eventually be adjacent to the Hong Kong landmass across from Shenzhen Bay.

People have come to make their fortune, and it reminds me of the historical accounts of men and women in America who moved out west to strike it rich. Modeling agents come to Shekou to seek out Western children and adults who are interested in being the "new face" of famous Chinese brands. Prostitutes do their work without any consideration of a moral code or proper conduct; to them, it is simply a job like any other, without emotional or physical attachments. Men who know that the majority of expatriates don't drive, stand and wait for people to request their private services. Many come and work, only to send their earnings to family members in other parts of China. It is a mixture of young and old, known and unknown, interesting and mundane.

Today, I used the back of an envelope to record the various items which I saw manually transported in carts, on bicycles, etc. I have stapled it into the journal: hens, eggs, barrels of water, tires, fish, pineapple, carrots, plants/shrubbery, plywood, bamboo poles, unknown fruit, potatoes, McDonalds delivery, pizza, dirt, bricks, sand, the roots of a tree, and people. I was outside for less than two hours. Ponder this.

Losing face in China is avoided at all costs. It is highly unlikely that a Chinese person will say that he/she is unable to do something. Typically, they would rather tell you that they can do something to your face and then let you know, later, that they cannot do whatever it was. Negotiating is highly acceptable, and many shops welcome the friendly banter surrounding requests for discounts or bargains. At times, the negotiation process can get loud. To a visitor, the discussion may appear to be an argument. It is not uncommon to hear a Western person ask, "Is he yelling?" with a Chinese person responding, "No, he's just talking loudly." Expatriate: "He seems to be yelling!" Chinese person: "No, don't worry. He's not angry; he's just talking." No one wants to be wrong, yet this seems to be a common international issue. It takes a mature person to admit insecurities, face the fact that he/she is wrong, and at times, apologize for shortcomings. But this is China, and one might think that losing face is the equivalent of losing a limb.

April 13 2009—No, you can't give in.

I needed to have some curtains made for our new apartment, so I gladly joined a bilingual friend of mine, Jen, and made the much-dreaded trip to a fabric market in Luohu. Although I use "much-dreaded" too loosely, as I simply have a difficult time trying to choose fabric in a place where there are at least four floors with countless bolts of material. A person could get lost in this fabric mall and have lifelong nightmares of being stuck inside. I imagine that this one building had at least (with no exaggeration) 100,000 bolts. Finally, after four hours of looking, I found exactly what I was looking for. Once I had committed to my decision, I explained the dimensions to Jen, and she began chatting with the saleslady.

As usual, the two began discussing the price and going back and forth in the negotiation process. Anywhere else, I know I would have been uncomfortable with the entire discourse, volume as well as body language. I would never dream of dickering with salespeople back home. However, at the end of their twenty-minute rampage, Jen looked at me and said, "Start walking." "Uhh . . . but, uhh . . . but . . . what about . . . ." I stammered. "Ssh! Just walk," said Jen. Within seconds, the saleslady had caught up with us, panting "*Hao. Hao. Hao.*" I looked over and saw that Jen had a triumphant grin on her face. She had won the negotiation battle, and I was the proud winner of new curtains. As the saleslady began to take measurements, I could see Jen's satisfaction. This had been a normal part of the game that is often played in stores. With excitement, the game continues until the victor, or the best bargainer wins.

As we left the fabric mall this afternoon, I asked Jen about the hand-gestures, which I have been wondering about for quite some time. The Chinese people can count to ten on one hand, as they create signals for the numbers six through ten. They do this because they often only have one hand free. I noticed it more frequently in the fabric mall, as many would hold a bolt in one hand while gesturing with the other. As we walked toward the *lao jie* metro station, she tried to teach me. Six was easy, as it is the same gesture Americans use for "hang loose," and seven actually looked like a seven. However, eight and nine were a bit more difficult to remember, and I am not sure if I could even recall them now, at the end of the day.

Jen shared some additional, interesting things regarding numbers. First, you will see that the numbers four and fourteen have often been omitted from many apartment complexes. She said that this is due to the fact that the number four, when pronounced in one of the other four tones, actually means death. Therefore, very few people want to be associated with the number four because the tones may be confused. (*Great*, I thought, *I am moving to the fourth building in a new apartment complex . . . how comforting!*) Second, Jen said that in Cantonese, which is the primary language in Hong Kong and Guangdong province, eight means wealth or good fortune. Therefore, eight is considered to be a lucky number. Many people want to have a phone number that includes the number eight or have children born on the eighth of the month, and so on. She also told me that Chinese do not like odd numbers, as someone is always left out. Even numbers are believed to be whole or complete. (*Oh, good*, I thought. *Four is an even number.*) Finally, if you call someone "two hundred fifty" in Mandarin, it is considered derogatory. I can only deduce that 250 is a quarter of a thousand, implying that one really only has a quarter of a brain. Who knows, but I won't be caught bargaining with a suggested price of 250 yuan any time soon!

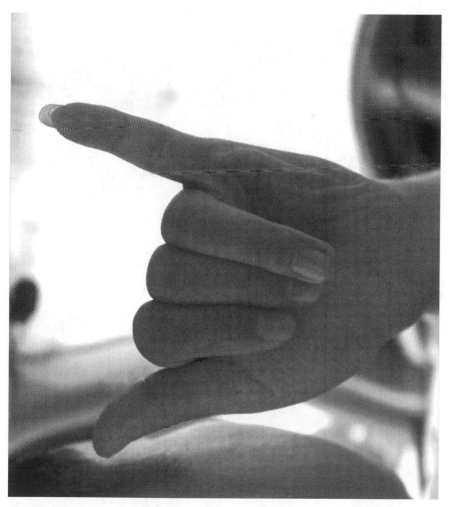

it costs 6 yuan . . . negotiation

mobile market

September 28, 2011 — 250 came to mind.

Today, I hired four men off the street. They moved four massive pieces of a solid wood bedroom suite into my apartment. They were slight in stature, yet brawny in ability. It took them less than one hour to disassemble, move from the first floor of one building to the thirtieth floor of another, and reassemble the furniture. As I pulled out my handbag to pay them, my first thought was to "give them 250," and then, my subconscious somehow pulled, "no, that would be an insult . . . . 350 it is." As I sit here and journal, I realize that it is not an insult. No, it is rather my mind that is beginning to remember various intricacies of cultural expectations and beliefs in China. Have I been here that long? How long would it take for me to feel as though I fit? Will I ever fit? If I go home, will I still feel as though I fit there? Have I changed so much that I won't recognize my own land? At one point, do we feel like an expatriate in every land? Will home always feel like home? The last time I got on the plane bound for Hong Kong, I looked to John and said, "When we get home . . ." I paused, cocked my head to the side, and smiled. *Where is my home?* Here, I record something that has held me fast: My true home is not on this Earth, rather in a place that has been prepared for me by my Heavenly Father. For those who believe, the promise of this eternal home brings more comfort and joy than any temporary dwellings of this life. Therefore, my heart is at peace.

The Reaction

Some have read this book and chuckled, while others may have read this book and scoffed. Some have read this book with doubt, and some have read this book with interest. Expatriates in Shenzhen have possibly read this book with an odd fondness and nostalgia. Whatever the feelings, it is a book that has inspired us to think about cultural implications and how we react to our environments. Regardless of age, gender, race, and nationality, we have all experienced the unknown, the unfamiliar in life. It is in these times that we grow and learn about diversity . . . and about ourselves. Diversity enhances the mind as it encourages us to think in a way that we may never have thought possible. In the midst of personal biases and generalizations, we discover that each and every culture is simply a patchwork of people, woven together to display a myriad of perspectives, experiences, and traditions. It is in these times that we learn the most. Having lived in China, I will never be the same; for this, I am grateful. It is a country that holds a unique place in my heart.

How has your home changed you, forever? If your response is "I don't know" or "I don't think it has," I challenge you to reflect. Think about how, consciously and subconsciously, those around you might have affected you. Why do you think the way that you do, and how have you come to think in this way?

September 19, 2011 — Where do you stand amid it all?

And just when I think I have had enough of the mannerisms and inconceivable behavior, a beacon amid the crowd appears. Tonight, I was standing in the rain with no umbrella. I was dressed in a black and white polka dot shirt, white shorts, and black, Teva flip-flops. A young man, quite tall by Chinese standards, passed me three times. He glanced my way, as if mustering the courage to talk to me, but he never spoke; he simply made his way to stand by my side and held his umbrella above me while I searched for a taxi. His gesture was silent, yet he spoke volumes. All I could manage to say was, *"xie xie."* He bowed his head in most humble acceptance, and I could see that his kindness was pure, like that of a sunrise, erupting, unnoticed to a sleeping world. In the midst of stereotypes, there are some who will "take the road less traveled," and their choices will never be forgotten. I do not know his name; it is lost among the millions. Tonight, I am thanking him and hoping that he feels the same warmth that I felt from his actions and his silence, both of which spoke volumes.

About the Author

Ruth N. Stevenson

With undergraduate studies in English as well as an MEd in Curriculum, Instruction, and Assessment, Ruth dedicates her life to researching, writing, teaching, and being taught. Before moving to China, she balanced being a middle school teacher, high school instructional coach, collegiate resident director, and doctoral studies student. She continued her teaching as an English consultant for two international companies. While in China, she opened Venture Abroad, LLC, which provides Chinese students with an opportunity to attend a comprehensive English summer-school program in the United States. She has been honored with a variety of awards, including the Paul Meek Leadership Award and the Teacher of the Year Award for her school district. In her spare time, she enjoys exploring, reading, and journaling. As a devoted wife and mother, Ruth's sincere desire is to witness cross-cultural and personal awareness come alive through the juxtaposition of art, exploration, and personal anecdotes.

About the Photographer

Natalia Segura

Natalia's undergraduate work in business prepared her to earn an MBA and work in the global market. While living in Europe, her marketing experience and multilingual advantage propelled her into management positions. Before relocating to China, Natalia lived and worked in Prague, where her innate skill as a photographer was unearthed. Since then, her work has been published in numerous professional newsletters as well as displayed at notable exhibitions throughout Asia. In her spare time, she enjoys traveling, reading, and socializing. As a dedicated wife and mother to three children, Natalia effectively balances life's demands. Her lifelong dream is to produce photos that inspire both internal and external reflection.